Leander Samuel Coan

Better in the Mornin'

Ballads of Pathos, Humor and Satire

Leander Samuel Coan

Better in the Mornin'
Ballads of Pathos, Humor and Satire

ISBN/EAN: 9783744794596

Printed in Europe, USA, Canada, Australia, Japan

Cover: Foto ©Thomas Meinert / pixelio.de

More available books at **www.hansebooks.com**

BETTER IN THE MORNIN'.

BALLADS

of

PATHOS, HUMOR, AND SATIRE,

BY

REV. LEANDER S. COAN.

"LET ME WRITE THE BALLADS OF A PEOPLE, AND I CARE NOT
WHO WRITES THEIR LAWS."

Great Falls, N. H.
EDWARD O. LORD AND COMPANY.
1880.

TO ALL WHO HAVE WEPT WITH ME IN SYMPATHY FOR

THE OLD CORPORAL IN HIS SORROW,

AND TO ALL WHO ARE LOYAL TO THE CAUSE IN WHICH HE WAS
MAIMED,

This Volume is Affectionately Dedicated

BY

THE AUTHOR.

For to-day I write with pen made sharp,

Though carping critics smile and carp;

Of yesterday write, though blinded by tears,

For hearing having neither haste nor fears;

For to-morrow, pen with patient thought,

With fear nothing, with malice naught;

With patience sow my seed, and then

Await the tears and smiles of men,

And strive no single word to trace

I might with tears wish to erase.

CONTENTS.

---◆◆◆---

EARLY POEMS.

PART III.

BIOGRAPHICAL SKETCH.

The author of these songs and ballads was the eldest son of Deacon Samuel Coan, of Garland, Maine; ·born in Exeter, Maine, November 17, 1837, and a direct descendant of Peter Coan, who came to America from Worms, Germany, in·1715. His ancestors, on the maternal side, traced their lineage directly back to the Pilgrims that came over in the "Mayflower."

His parents, belonging to the humbler walks of life, were by no means lacking in intelligence, and they sought to give their children that which would stand them in hand better than the wealth which they could not bestow,— an education and an honest name. His early life was spent in the common and high schools of the towns of Exeter and Garland.

At a very early age he showed a strong inclination to become a preacher, and while yet very young would return from church and preach the sermon he had heard over again to his parents and relatives; going through the whole sermon with great solemnity, using his own words, however, but words very apt and accurate to the subject.

Later on in life he fell in with associates who were believers in liberal doctrines, and for a time he was afloat upon the sea of scepticism and doubt. At the age of twenty, while engaged in teaching at Brewer Village, Maine, he experienced a sudden radical change in his views upon religion, and became a working, sterling Christian. A few months previous to this change he had settled upon the law as his profession, and went to Bangor to study with Ex-Governor Kent ; but, finding himself deficient in some of the languages, decided to take private instructions in them and teach school for a while. His conversion, like Paul's, made a complete revolution in his life, and he soon determined to preach the " Gospel of the Blessed Master."

Finishing his theological studies, he was graduated from the Theological Seminary at Bangor, Maine, in the summer of 1862. Supplying the Congregational Church at Amherst, Maine, until the summer of 1863, he was ordained over that church and remained until the spring of 1864, when he spent his vacation in Cohasset, Mass. In August, 1864, his long pent-up patriotism burst the bounds that had confined him, and he enlisted as a private in the Sixty-first Massachusetts Volunteers, with the promise that, when the battalion of six companies was increased to a full regiment, entitling them to a chaplain, he should have that position. Meantime he acted as chaplain for his battalion, and as the war drew near its close, and no more men were required, his regiment was never filled, and consequently he was not commissioned chaplain. After the war he preached at Boothbay, Me., three years, Brownville, Me., three years, Bradford, Me., six months, Somerset and Fall River, Mass., above three years, and Alton, N.H., about five years. He began to write verses not far from 1860, and about the first piece was entitled "Change the Figures." "The Reply of Night" and "Morning in Spring-time" were written not far from this time.

The last piece of the " Old Corporal Series" was written a few days before the State election in Maine, which took place

September 8, 1879. The piece was entitled " Fall In." I think, if he had been spared until the present writing, January 15, 1880, that the Old Corporal's wooden leg would have come down with more " vicious vim" than when he heard of Hill's speech in Congress.

I can do no better than to quote an obituary in the editorial columns of the " Independent Statesman," published at Concord, N.H., a short time after his death. The lyric referred to was the " Soldier's Farewell," and was his last effort.

DEATH OF REV. LEANDER S. COAN.

By a postal card, thoughtfully forwarded by Commander C. J. Richards, Past Commander, Department of New Hampshire, Grand Army of the Republic, we have received the sorrowful intelligence of the death, on Wednesday morning, at his residence in Alton, of Rev. Leander S. Coan, better known to our readers as the author of the Old Corporal Ballads, most of which were first given to the public in these columns. Although he was known to have been for some time in poor health, and latterly quite ill, his friends at a distance were totally unprepared to hear of his demise. In the prime of life, and apparently of a rugged constitution, being compactly built, with broad shoulders, large, well-poised head and a ruddy countenance, beaming always with good nature, he seemed destined to a long life.

Only a few days since — September 16 — we received a note from him, enclosing the poem which we published last week, entitled " The Soldier's Farewell," which is so characteristic of the man and the true soldier of the Union and of the Cross, that we give it here verbatim : —

" FRIEND STEVENS : Please find a little lyric enclosed. I would rather have my name at the foot of the piece than over it, so have erased it there.

" Was sick in bed and couldn't get to Manchester. Guess I will die, but will die *game*. Yours, PARSON."

Our readers are aware that in the series of ballads the author referred to himself as the " Parson," and in many of his private notes to us he used that signature. Mr. Coan was a man of ardent temperament and strong feelings, without being in the least fanatical or dogmatic. A Union soldier in the war of the rebellion, he was proud of his record as such and intensely patriotic. A member of the G.A.R. he took a lively interest in all that pertained to the order, and filled many posts of honor in it, always to the acceptance of his comrades. A clergyman of the Congregational denomination, he was also active in all movements for the advancement of the cause of humanity, laboring assiduously with voice and pen for the promotion of temperance, good government, and morality. With poetical gifts of no inferior order, he used them always in furtherance of the good of his brother-man. He wrote, whether in prose or rhyme, out of a full heart and for a worthy purpose. Our columns have been enriched by his contributions in metrical verse and an occasional prose sketch. He also acted as our news correspondent, and wrote more or less for other journals, and for magazines. He was a hard-working man, and, with a large family dependent upon him, this was a necessity. Besides his literary labors and his work as a pastor, he lectured frequently before lyceums and temperance organizations, adding thus to his meagre pittance as a pastor settled over a small society.

His poems have had a wide circulation, many of them having been extensively copied by the newspaper press of the country. Perhaps the most admired of his metrical effusions is the plaintive poem entitled "Better in the Mornin'." An earnest believer in Republican principles, and a foe to oppression in every form, many of his Old Corporal Ballads are directed against the attempts to reverse the results of the war, and are stinging rebukes to the flunky spirit which gained such headway during and subsequent to the late presidential campaign. Of these "Hill's Brigade" is the most spirited. Some of his battle-pieces are dramatic and realistic, as would naturally be the case with one who has himself participated in the conflict of arms. For some time past Mr. Coan has been engaged in collecting and revising his poems, with a view to their publication in book form, and the last time we saw him he told us of his plans, which were then nearly perfected, for bringing out the book. We believe it is now going through the press. We hope so; and trust that it may have a wide sale, not alone because of its merits, and its excellent inculcations, but because it will be a godsend to his widow and little children, who are left with only very limited means of support.

Mr. Coan had his faults — and who has not? He was somewhat erratic in his ideas, and too sensitive, perhaps, to public praise or censure. But he was warm-hearted, true to his convictions, and without cant or bigotry. As a friend and comrade he will be greatly missed by the boys who wore the blue, for whom he had an abiding affection, which grew with the lapse of time.

He had been out of health for nearly a year, but his physicians had not thought his case a critical one ; consequently his death came with a terrible suddenness to his friends and relatives. His funeral occurred September 27th, in the church he had labored in for five years, conducted by the Masons, of whose order he was an enthusiastic member. The ceremony was very impressive, especially that at the grave, when the whispering pines in the background and the mellow autumn sunlight softened the senses and hallowed the spot forever to some of us. I wish to add my tribute to his memory here on these pages. I must confess that I was never so enthusiastic in regard to his writings as he wished me to be, and I will only say in excuse that I never saw his sweetest songs until after he had been transferred to the Grand Army beyond the River. As I was perusing some of the gems contained in this volume, I chanced to take up the Gospel Hymns No. 2, and read these lines, —

" Strange we never prize the music
Till the sweet-voiced bird is flown."

I would have given worlds if I had had them at my command at that moment to have had him back with us just for one hour.

E. S. COAN, M.D.

GARLAND, January 15, 1880.

PART I.

PART I.

INTRODUCTION.

The Corporal, ladies and gentlemen,
  Allow me, if you please,
To present him, and vouch for,
  From reasons such as these:
I have known him as friend and comrade
  Before and during the war,
And since as neighbor and brother,
  In all worth vouching for.

He never betrayed a secret, —
  He never deserted a friend;
And upon just what he tells you
  You safely may depend.
Stalwart, staunch, and honest,
  To his conscience true to the end,
In all of life's relations
  Ennobling the name of friend.

Often uncouth in expression,
  Yet his meaning is terse and tense;
And I have never found him
  Lacking in good sound sense.

He stands as a type of many
  Whom you, perhaps, have known;
And whatever he utters, you safely
  May reckon to be his own.

In lodge, post, march, and bivouac,
  I have sat, and messed with him, too,
And in all I have ever found him
  Loyal, and stanch, and true;
And I hope, when life's march is over,
  To meet with and greet him again,
When the Lord shall call the honor'd roll
  Of NEW ENGLAND common men.

And though but two stripes on blue-blous'd arm
  Give sign of his rank below,
His heart deserves a General's star,
  As we who knew him know;
And when the hosts are gathered
  In the Lord Christ's grand review,
Perhaps he then will wear a star,
  In those legions loyal too.

And I hope, in the streets of the city
  Said to be paved with gold,
To hear (on the mellow pave ringing,
  As in, then to be, days of old)
His step and voice so cheerful;
  And this boon I will beg:
That God will there permit him to wear
  The badge of a wooden leg.

                              THE PARSON.

OLD CORPORAL POEMS.

———•◦•———

BETTER IN THE MORNIN'.

" You can't help the baby, parson,
  But still I want you to go
Down and look in upon her,
  An' read and pray, you know.
Only last week she was skippin' round,
  A-pullin' my whiskers an' hair,
A-climbin' up to the table
  Into her little high chair.

" The first night that she took it,
  When her little cheeks grew red,
When she kissed good-night to papa,
  And went away to bed,
Sez she, '' 'Tis headache, papa,
  Be better in mornin' — bye '!
An' somthin' in how she said it
  Jest made me want to cry.

" But the mornin' brought the fever,
  An' her little hands grew hot,
An' the pretty red uv her little cheeks
  Grew into a crimson spot.
But she lay there jest ez patient
  Ez ever a woman could,
Takin' whatever we gave her
  Better'n a grown woman would.

"The days are terrible long an' slow,
    An' she's grown wuss in each;
An' now she's jest a slippin'
    Clear away out uv our reach.
Every night when I kiss her,
Tryin' hard not to cry,
    She says in a way that kills me —
        'Be better in mornin' — bye'!

"She can't get through the night, parson,
    So I want ye to come an' pray,
An' talk with mother a little, —
    You'll know jest what to say;
Not that the baby needs it,
    Nor that we make any complaint
That God seems to think he's needin'
    The smile uv the little saint."

*   *   *   *   *   *   *   *

I walked along with the Corporal
    To the door of his humble home,
To which the silent messenger
    Before me had also come;
And if he had been a titled prince
    I would not have been honored more
Than I was with his heart-felt welcome
    To his lowly cottage door.

Night falls again in the cottage;
    They move in silence and dread
Around the room where the baby
    Lies panting upon her bed.
"Does baby know papa, darling?"
    And she moves her little face
With answer that shows she knows him;
    But scarce a visible trace

Of her wonderful infantile beauty
    Remains as it was before

The unseen silent messenger
    Had waited at their door.
"Papa — kiss — baby.   I's *so* tired!"
    The man bows low his face,
And two swollen hands are lifted
    In baby's last embrace.

And into her father's grizzled beard
    The little red fingers cling,
While her husky, whispered tenderness
    Tears from a rock would bring.
"Baby — is — *so* — sick — papa —
    But — don't — want — you — to cry;"
The little hand falls on the coverlet —
    Be — *better* — in — mornin' — bye!"

And night around baby is falling,
    Settling down dark and dense;
Does God need their darling in heaven
    That he must carry her hence,
I prayed with tears in my voice,
    As the Corporal solemnly knelt,
With grief such as never before
    His great warm heart had felt.

O frivolous men and women!
    Do you know that round you and night,
Alike from the humble and haughty,
    Goeth up evermore the cry,
"My child! my precious! my darling!
    How *can* I let you die!"
Oh, hear ye the white lips whisper:
    "Be — better — in — mornin' — bye!"

1876.

TEARS OF JOY.

"Thank God, parson, with me now,
　　That the baby is better *here;*
Better in earthly morning;
　　That still her voice we hear.
I thought when she was a-layin'
　　So quiet, an' sick, an' still,
Can it be that God wants *this* one?
　　Could I submit to his will?

"An' thought while I watched her so careful,
　　Through tryin' nights an' days,
Uv the one who in heaven's mornin'
　　Is singin' their hymns uv praise.
An' my heart was heavy an' fearful,
　　My eyes were hot an' dry,
I couldn't see how I could bear it
　　To have this little one die.

"She had filled up the place that was empty,
　　At the table an' in our hearts,
An' had grown around us so closely
　　With her sweet little ways an' arts,
That it seemed ez if it would kill me
　　To stan' by an' see her die, —
To think uv *her* hands folded
　　An' kissin' us all good-by,

"Ez our sweet little pet you remember
　　So tenderly did before,
When the ' unseen silent messenger
　　Waited at our door.'
I think God knew that we couldn't
　　Bear it again, an' so
On our dumb fear took pity,
　　Concludin' she needn't go.

" Ez I could only thank him
    Ez it's in my heart to do ; —
But there ! He knows all about it,
    Ef the good book tells us true,
That there isn't a single sparrow
    That flutters an' blindly falls,
But He takes notice uv it !
    He *must* hear the cry that calls

" For pity an' mercy in trouble ;
    An' it must be pleasant for Him,
When he can do what we ask Him,
    So our faith won't get too dim.
An' ef ever I get into heaven
    The first thing that I'll do,
Will be to thank Him that this time
    He brought the baby through,

" Without concludin' He needed her
    With Him jest yet up there.
I think he must have noticed
    The tears that wer' in my prayer !
They weren't nowhere else, that's certain,
    For my eyes wer' hot an' dry ;
But I think he must have noticed
    In my heart a fearful cry.

" So I want you to thank Him for me,
    An' tell Him just how I feel,
For I can't begin to explain it
    Though I try to when I kneel.
Why, just see the sweet little precious
    Runnin' and playin' about,
A-fillin' the house with sunshine
    An' the joy uv the playful shout !

" Come here an' kiss papa, sweet one ;
    His heart thanks God to-day

(Though you know little about it)
    That the Lord could let you stay.
I think ef God takes notice
    In heaven's tearless days
Uv the joy he sometimes gives us
    He will find that his pity pays.

" I can't see how he helps cryin'
    When he looks down 'n' sees
The joy it gives to have them
    A-patterin' round our knees,
/When we have been weepin' over them
    In fear that they might go,
When they just seemed to be driftin'
    Away from us sure an' slow."

And I have thought with the Corporal:
    There is something in the plan
That gives to the throne in heaven
    The heart of the Son of Man.
Yes, He who to-day, and yesterday,
    And forever is the same,
Weeping from joy at our happiness
    Gives heaven another claim

To our love and loyal devotion
    To One who knows and feels
The heart's unutterable anguish
    When a trembling pleader kneels.
And I think that the Corporal's fancy
    Of God's sympathetic tears
Finds blessed confirmation
    In the Intercessor's years.

1878.

THE GOOD OLD FARM.

" There's got to be a revival
    Uv good sound sense among men,
Before the days uv prosperity
    Will dawn upon us again.
The boys must learn that learnin'
    Means more'n the essence uv books ;
An' the girls must learn that beauty
    Consists in more'n their looks.

" Ef the boys all grow up savants,
    Studyin' rocks 'n' bugs,
An' the girls grow up blue-stockin's
    Or experts in kisses 'n' hugs, —
Who'll keep the old plow in order,
    Or fix up the traces 'n' tugs ;
Who'll sweep the floor uv the kitchen,
    Or weave up the carpets 'n' rugs?

" Before we can steer clear uv failures,
    An' big financial alarms,
The boys have got to quit clerkin'
    An' git back onto the farms.
I know it aint quite so nobby,
    It aint quite so *easy*, I know,
Ez partin' yer hair 'n the middle
    An' settin' up for a show.

" But there's more hard dollars in it,
    An' more independence, too,
An' more real peace 'n' contentment,
    An' health that's ruddy an' true.
I know it takes years uv labor,
    But yu've got to ' hang on ' in a store
Before you can earn a good livin'
    An' clothes, with but little more.

" An' yer steer well clear uv temptation
   On the good old honest farm,
An' a thousand ways 'n' fashions
   That only brings ye to harm.
There aint but a few that can handle,
   With safety, other men's cash,
An' the fate uv many who try it
   Proves human natur' is rash.

" So, when the road to State's-prison
   Lays by the good old farm,
An' the man sees a toilin' brother
   Well out uv the way uv harm,
He mourns 't he hadn't staid there,
   A-tillin' the soil in peace,
Where he'll yet creep back in dishonor
   After a tardy release.

" What hosts uv 'em go back, broken
   In health, 'n' mind, 'n' purse,
To die in sight uv the clover,
   Or linger along, which is worse !
An' how many mourn when useless
   That they didn't see the charm,
The safety 'n' independence,   .
   Uv a life on the good old farm.

" So preach it up to 'em, parson,
   Jest lay it out plain 'n' square,
That land flows with milk 'n' honey,
   That health 'n' peace are there.
An' call back the clerks 'n' runners
   An' show 'em the peace 'n' charm
That waits to cheer an' bless them,
   On father's dear old farm."

The Corporal's farm bears witness,
   His cottage is snug and trim,

The failures and embezzlements
　　Have no "hard times" for him.
Long may he live to enjoy it,
　　Free from financial harm,
A true New England nobleman,
　　Who thinks, while tilling his farm.

————o○◦◦◦○o————   ·

THE OLD CORPORAL MARKS THE PERFECT MAN.

"He has been to my house, parson,
　　A-peddlin' the Holy Book,
An' speakin' a word ag'in him
　　Won't have a kindly look.
But he says he *haint sinned*, parson,
　　In *deed*, nor even *thought*,
For risin' eight year, nor had a *wish*
　　But what a Christian ought!

"So I'm afeard uv him, parson,
　　He's so awful, terrible good;
For he goes braggin' about it,
　　Ez a humble man never would.
I think that bein' perfect,
　　Aint a thing to be boastin' about;
It won't make a man obtrusive
　　For fear we won't find it out.

"Ef a man is so near the blessed light
　　Uv the everlastin' sun,
You cannot fail to be convinced
　　Uv the glorious work that's done.
An' he won't be blowin' about it,
　　Like the painter I think uv now,

Who had to write, under a doubtful daub,
   'This animal is a cow!'

"Ef he hadn't *claimed* to be perfect,
   I sartinly shouldn't have guessed
That his life would level up higher·
   Or better than the rest.
So I'm jest a goin' ter *mark him*
   (Its scriptural, so I can),
For, don't the good book tell us
   To 'mark the perfect man'?

"He haint learned the grace uv modesty,
   Nor uv mindin' his own concerns;
Nor the grace uv a charitable sperrit;
   Nor that spinnin' tattling yarns
Don't jibe well with his wonderful claim
   Uv not havin' sinned for years,
And for these, an' *other reasons*,
   I have for his truthfulness, fears.

"Ef he's perfect, this mark won't hurt him;
   He'll only shine more bright;
An' the town where he lives will be noted
   For havin' a shinin' light.
An' agin, ef he's really perfect,
   Readin' this he won't be mad,
But,·for an onerate sinner,
   Will be only a trifle sad."

Cut this out, and if you see him
   In the daylight or in the dark,
Just look him carefully over,
   To find the Corporal's mark.
Take this truth (in a nut-shell),
   On which good sense relies:
The man who *claims to be sinless*
   Is foolish, or he lies.

THE OLD CORPORAL'S MITE.

" There's a dollar, parson,
　　An' I want to have it go
For the forefather's monument,
　　Which seems to be risin' slow.
The year that I enlisted
　　I tried to get down to the place,
To see where they landed and wintered,
　　For I belong to their race.

" But I couldn't get a furlough
　　To run down, not for a day ;
An' somehow it slipped my memory
　　After I marched away.
An' so many things have happened,
　　The losin' uv my leg,
An' stumpin' around these many years
　　On this ere wooden peg, —

" I somehow forgot they were buildin'
　　A monument down there,
So I never yet have given
　　What I may call my share.
We can't afford to forget them !
　　It will pay us well to build
In memory uv the fathers who
　　Gave us the soil we've tilled.

" An' they gave us a sight more, parson,
　　Ef our eyes were open to see !
They died a-foundin' a nation,
　　Ez we fought to keep it free.
When I think uv their freezin' in winter,
　　An' starvin' when crops were poor,
An' fightin' the savage Indians,
　　An' the fate that seemed so sure,

" Standin' there. bold an' unflinchin',
    Ez firm ez their Plymouth Rock,
Pestilence thinnin' the number
    Uv the little undaunted flock ;
Or think uv their places of worship,
    Uv the hardships they underwent,
I think we have good reason
    To thank them, an' be content.

" An' I just feel ashamed to murmur,
    Ez I'm sometimes tempted to do,
When I think uv what they suffered,
    An' what they all went through.
Where would be Yale or Harvard,
    An' the shaft at Bunker Hill,
Ef they had been lacking in conscience,
    Or muscle, or pluck, or will ?

" Ef they'd lacked religi'n an' learnin',
    I've been askin myself uv late,
Could they have planned a Nation,
    Or planted the seed uv a State ?
Where would be Boston 'n Chicago,
    Ef they had failed to stand ?
An' where the flag that's floatin'
    In peace over all the land ?

" Each year we give for monuments,
    For far less deserving men ;
Fly buntin' an' burn powder
    On Fourth of July, an' then
Complete, but only on paper,
    A monumental *plan*,
For the man who died a foundin'
    A Race, on the Rights uv Man.

" An' I won't neglect it longer,
    So here's the dollar for me ;

I'll stump round 'n' earn another,
    For those who kept it free !
I can save for such noble offerings,
    Ef I do wear a wooden leg ;
Ef all felt this ez they ought to
    The cause wouldn't have to beg."

So accept the old corporal's offering,
    For the monument on the shore,
Where now as when they landed
    Atlantic surges roar.
And while the sun shines or storm-clouds
    Shall darken our changing skies,
May it stand complete and sacred
    In other Pilgrim eyes.

And loyal to conscience and duty,
    May they tread the hallowed sod,
Where rests the dust of heroes,
    Freemen and men of God.
May we keep alive the lessons
    Their lives and valor teach,
So long as our race has being,
    And freedom of thought and speech.

ACROSS THE CHASM.

"It reads like a nightmare, parson,
    The way they've been dying, down South,
At Memphis an' all them places !
    I've been rather rough with my mouth,
Ag'in some of them sassy ex-rebels :
    But my heart has never been cold :

An' I'm ready to help 'em in trouble,
    With ice, food, clothing, or gold.

"It has made my heart ache for our brothers
  ' That are dying a hunderd a day,
Without nurses, or ice, or blankets,
    The tide uv the scourge ter stay,
My heart has grown warm towards 'em,
    An' I'm glad that we're able ter show
That in times ov sich terrible trouble
    No North or South we know.

"So, over the bloody chasm,
    Rent by the Rebel war,
We've held out our hands ter give 'em
    Things they were dying for,
It'll be just ag'in all natur'
    Be that natur' white or black,
Ef a wave ov warm Southern gratitude
    Doosn't come surgin' back."

God grant that this expression
    Of the warmth of the Northern heart,
A wave of brotherly welcome
    From the stricken South may start.
We will meet it, and gladly greet it
    As a sign of better days, —
A breath of fate may scatter
    The mists, the battle's haze.

So, clasping hands and kindly
    Looking into each other's eyes,
May a new fraternity rising,
    Fill all with glad surprise.
The lessons of war have taught us
    The hand of a foe to respect:
May the lessons of peace and sufferings
    The love of our hearts reflect.

Until all doubt and dissension
  Forever shall disappear,
As the arching dome of the Union
  Cemented with love we rear;
And when that dome is completed,
  Both North and South may it span,
Until humble and haughty acknowledge
  The brotherhood of man.

Though they believed not, nor thought it;
  For this we have stood, and have fought;
Then, with arms we taught it,
  And now, with our alms have taught,
God grant that aright they read it,
  In this hour of stricken woe;
That we and they may heed it,
  And the fruit of fraternity grow.

Often uncouth the expressions
  I bring from my soldier friend,
The Corporal, yet I repeat him,
  And trust that in the end,
His words shall bear for justice
  And equal rights for all,
Whether war, with its clarion summons,
  Or charity tenderly call.

THE OLD CORPORAL ON BARRON.

"Didn't you write up, parson,
    Mr. Barron, your old-time friend?
An' what do *you* think uv the 'theory,'
    That his own hand sought his end?
Is your martyr an' hero to tumble
    From that eminence so high,
Where, at 'the Post of Duty
    He was ready an' strong to die'?"

Yes, comrade, I wrote and repeat it;
    There is not one word to unsay.
Of old, such ghouls of the Master
    Said, "They came and stole him away."
Are those *wonderful* detectives
    Quickened by hope of reward?
And are those tardy doctors
    Standing in sweet accord?

He must have had genius like Dante,
    Or Dickens, or grand Shakespeare,
To plan out that plot and details,
    Which seemed to run so clear,
And hushed all thoughts of suspicion
    Until almost a year
Had wreathed his brow with a halo
    That gleamed out grand and clear.

You may well ask who *are* they,
    And what are their ultimate aims?
Who, and what stands back of this theory
    Which a dead man's honor defames?
And what shall rise up to hinder
    The claim we next shall hear?
Will it be the reward for finding
    Who murdered the dead cashier?

Like the Prince of all patient martyrs,
  He stands while malice adorns
Under the radiant halo
  With the still cruel crown of thorns.
Thank God his pure brow feels not
  The touch of grave-robbing hands ;
And now our just indignation
  Before the accuser stands ;

To ask in the name of honor
  And justice, and all things fair,
That they prove beyond a cavil,
  Clear as the noonday air,
Beyond all doubt or question,
  Or stand for all time,
Like the Master's selfish accusers,
  Damned by a double crime.

Who are these ghouls that are digging
  At the grave of our dead cashier?
Some motive unseen impels them !
  The real red hand may be here —
Some one will gain, if this falsehood
  Gain credence and stand as true.
These men and their motives
  We propose to pierce through and through.

We call them now to answer ;
  They live, and may defend
Against the charge that they rest behind
  Some base and selfish end.
We will not wait till the silence
  Of death has sealed their lips,
Before we cast on *their* honor
  The doubt of a damning eclipse.

THE OLD CORPORAL ON WOOD AND COAL.

"I woke up the other night, parson,
   A-hearin' the cold wind blow,
A-howlin' around my dwellin'
   Drivin' the driftin' snow,
An' I thought of the poor folks, parson,
   Who haint got so much ez we ;
Who haint got no work nor money ; —
   Got to thinkin' how 'twould be

Ef I hadn't clothin' sufficient,
   Ef I hadn't wood nor coal,
Nor a bed that wuz warm and decent,
   Nor a shoe that wuz dry an' whole ; —
'N' I shuddered with only the thinkin',
   Tucked up nice an' warm ;
Thinkin' about the people
   A-sufferin' in the storm.

"'N' I thought uv 'em sick an' hungry,
   Thought uv 'em dyin' an' dead ;
An' thinkin' uv New Years an' Christmas,
   An' what the good Lord said
About bein' alwus with us ; —
   Though the meanin' uv that is dim
The other is plain an' simple,
   'Bout doin' it unto him.

"An' I just laid awake, thinkin',
   A'most the livelong night,
Turnin' it over and over,
   An' tryin' to get it right.
But I couldn't fix it nohow,
   To make it foot up square —
The way that things is divided
   Seems anything but fair.

" Why, there's that old man Stingy,
    Who never did anything good,
Who never did *anything* honest, —
    I don't think he ever would, —
Surrounded with wealth an' comfort,
    A sight too ugly to die,
So fat an' sleek an' happy ! —
    Can't see the reason why.

" But the widder Joneses children,
    So modest an' good an' kind ;
An' she is proper an' upright
    Ez any that you can find :
An' her husband was upright an' honest,
    Nor was he afeared to die ; —
Seein' them cold an' hungry, —
    I *can't* see the reason why,

" Except that they're alwus with us
    To give us a chance to give,
While showin' the terrible trouble
    Through which some folks can live ;
Showin' how patient an' thankful
    All uv us ought to be,
To make us kind to the people
    Who haint got so much ez we.

" There's poor little Tim McPeters
    A-coughin' his life away,
Who ought to be out a-slidin' —
    Jest the right age to play ;
Sick, yet patient an' thankful,
    Without any grapes or beef,
A-hoverin' over a broken stove
    With no hope — no relief.

" We can give 'em some wood to warm 'em,
    We can give 'em a loaf uv bread,

An' pull over the stuff in the attic
  To find a quilt for the bed.
'Twould be a shame an' a pity
  To see the poor boy dead,
Without any wood for a fire,
  An' not enough on the bed.

" Can't *you* think uv somethin', parson,
  Can't you think uv somethin' to *do*,
To stir up the wealthy people
  To help the poor folks through?
There's many uv 'em sick an' needy
  Without any fault uv theirs.
Can't you kind uv hint to the rich folk
  That *wood* 'll warm up their prayers?

" That when they set down by the bedside
  An' take a sick child's hand,
An' leave a smile fur cumfort,
  Along uv the *jell* on the stand,
An' hear the child's ' God bless ye ! '
  A-wipin' away the tears,
They're layin' up treasures an' riches
  Fur the best uv heaven's years !"

The Corporal paused, could say no more,
  His heart was all too full ;
It seemed as though it would burst and break
  Beneath his jacket of wool.
So here's my hand, old comrade,
  My heart and my pen to-day,
To speak your generous counsel
  For the Lord Christ's Christmas day.

CALEB WINN.

One day, as I sat in my study,
   I heard on the gravelled walk
A step which to me was familiar,
   But I missed the familiar talk, —
The Corporal's Yankee lingo,—
   So I knew that something was wrong,
For the old fellow's cheery accents
   Were never silent long.

" I want ye to come with me, parson,
   Down to see comrade Winn ;
He was with me in my regiment,
   An' the best uv neighbors has been.
He is sick an' in great trouble,
   An' wants to talk with you ;
You'll find whatever he tells ye,
   Like the gospel, straight an' true.

" He haint told me about it,
   So I think it's somethin' sad ;
He has taken his bed, an' wild-like,
   Takin' on terrible bad ;
His old wooden leg is hangin'
   Agin the bedroom wall ;
For you he keeps enquirin',
   But don't want others to call.

" Here we are at his cottage :
   Don't knock, but go right in ;
I'll wait here in the kitchen,
   Where I have often been ;
I hope you can help him somehow,
   I reckon it's caused by grief,
For he says that the doctors
   Can't give *him* any relief.

      *   *   *   *   *

" I'm reported in hospital, chaplain,
    And my time here is short,
But I'm not goin' to whinin',—
    You know I aint that sort;
Ever sence that day in the Wilderness
    I've been prest here, the heart;
Sence I lost my leg by a minnie,
    Couldn't stan' no great start.

" And now I've had one, chaplain,
    I'm sure I'm almost done;
This shot's goin' ter drop me,
    I've got ter turn in my gun.
When I knew that I was goin',
    That my march was almost through,
I thought that I might die easier
    Ef I could tell it ter you.

" No, *no* — 'taint *that*, chaplain,
    I fixt that long ago.
An' now, ef the Captain's ready,
    Then I'm all ready ter go.
I know that I'm fur from perfect,
    But I've been a-tryin' for years;
And 'bout that comin' roll-call
    I haint got any fears.

" It's about my daughter Mary,
    Who cried so when I went;
Who grew so tall 'n' han'some,
    So patient 'n' content;
How good a girl she's alwus been,
    How fair she's grown to be;
How kind she's been, and faithful,
    An' sot the world by me!

" O God! I can't tell it to ye!
    It came I don't know how,

But it's here, the wust of trouble,
   With no help for it now.
But he came so proper an' pleasin',
   He seemed to love her too ;
I'd ez soon have thought uv watchin'
   Or gone ter mistrustin' you.

" But the wust uv it is he's left her,
   And she's gone well-nigh mad ;
It breaks my heart to see her ;
   You know the smile she had, —
She sits now with a kind uv stare,
   That's jest heart-breakin' ter see ;
She don't know't I'm dyin',
   No, sir, she don't know me !

" You needn't tell me 'bout *law for it!*
   A hell, or a God, or not,
Ef there's any sich thing ez jestice,
   The villain ought ter be shot !
Ez I hope fur heaven, I'd do it,
   An' think I wuz doin' well ;
An' ef God knows a father's feelin's
   Be runnin' small resk uv hell.

" Some folks sez that ther' aint none !
   But what's ter be done with sich?
Where else can ther' be jestice
   For one like *him,* that's rich ?
Ef ther' aint none, then ther' should be,
   I guess that there'll be enough ;
An' fur sich fair-seemin' scoundrels,
   God can't make it too rough.

" Don't set there mutterin' ' *law* for it ' !
   What chance can ther' be in law ?
Can ye show me a case uv jestice
   In that way't ever ye saw ?

What chance ter bring back honor,
  Or innocence back again,
Or wipe from an honest family
  The least uv an awful stain?

"Why, he goes abroad respected,
  While she's ez good ez dead;
An' byme-by he'll be back ag'in,
  A-holdin' up his head.
But ef I could live ter see him here, —
  A Jedgment Day, or not, —
Ef his gravestone told the truth on it,
  'Twould say, 'The Villain was shot.'

"Been—weeks—has it—chaplain?
  Ye—see—I'm—goin' fast,
I want—you—to stay here—with me;
  It's comin'—discharge—at last.
I hope—that—Christ—will—remember,
  When—he—makes up the books,
The—blood—I shed—in battle,
  He—knows—how your own blood looks.

"Is—it night—now—or evenin'?" —
  "No, comrade, the sun shines clear." —
"Then—that—roll-call—is—comin',
  P'raps—you—can hear it—here,—
Dress by the colors!"   He wanders.
  "Could—I have—a flag—for a pall?
It seems—I can—see—one—floating
  From a flag-staff—grand and tall.

"It seems—to float—clear to heaven,
  Hark!—can I—hear—a bell?
Yes—it's—still—a-ringin'—
  You—cannot—hear it?—Well,
Good-by—take—care—uv—Mary—"
  And when he heard the roll,

I trust that Christ had mercy
   On the rough old soldier's soul.

And there on the wall of his bedroom,
   Hung up by its straps to a peg,
Just where he last had left it,
   Was his well-worn wooden leg.
We buried it carefully with him,
   Strapped on as it was before,
With the flag, as he requested,
   For none deserved it more.

And while I live and remember,
   I never can forget
His chivalric honor and "jestice,"
   Nor how his cheeks were wet
At the thought of the flag and Mary,
   Nor the treason he fought so well,
Nor the treason to woman's trust and love,
   By which at last he fell.

THE CORPORAL TO THE PARSON.

[Written by the author a few months before his decease.]

"Come, open yer heart to me, parson,
   What makes yer face so sad?
You've always been kind in my troubles,
   All that I've ever had.
An' now ef the thing is reversed like,
   An' yer need a helpin' hand,
I'm one that'll be found loyal,
   Close by your side to stand."

This is all that it is, corporal :
   My strength has been ebbing away ;
My hope and my courage have fallen,
   As life's power slipped away ;
And right in the midst of toiling,
   Right under a noon-day sun,
I feel that the day is ended,
   That my work and struggles are done.

I've got to lie down in the harness, —
   To give up and cease to vie
With athletic or any striver —
   Resigned and willing to die.
But while your words are powerless
   To lift the load I bare,
I could bless you to God forever,
   With kindest wish and prayer,

For seeing under cheeks that are paling,
   What baffles the healer's art, —
That something was wearing slowly away
   The strength of one beating heart.
And I will bless, and bless you ever
   For the kind words you have said,
For speaking the words sympathetic
   I would yearn for, even though dead.

POLITICAL.

HILL'S BRIGADE.

"Comrade, I've been mad to-day,
 Nigh mad enough to swear,
Thinkin' about the war 'n' the South,
 An' all we suffered there.
Those four long years, the dead we left,
 An' those who come home to die,
Uv what we fought an' hoped for —
 Mad with good reason why!

"I can't forgit they wer' rebels, —
 That this was their General Hill!
We have heard their yells afore;
 It seems I can hear them still.
To think uv that yell in Congress!
 Wal, let us 'move back the hands!
He boastin' uv 'father's' house, while
 No thanks to him it stands!

"Yes, lifted his hand ag'in' it,
 An' sot it well on fire!
An' knocked out the underpinin',
 Or, at least, 'twas his desire;
An' when 'father' caught and cuffed him,
 Lettin' him up with half enough, —
To come back so crank and sassy
 Is a-usin' the old man rough.

"Then there's that ' Wilkes Booth Hambleton ' !
    Doughfaces a-crawlin' back
To obey their old-time masters,
    An' hear the slave-whip crack !
Centennial !   Wal, I'm for it ;
    An' peace, an' good-will, an' such ;
But it seems they're askin' uv us
    Just a leetle too much.

"Ther's Gettysburg an' Antietam,
    The horrid Wilderness, too ;
Fort Pillow, Macon, an' Andersonville,
    With Wirtz an' his wicked crew.
An' we've got to knuckle at last, —
    To swaller our shame an' chagrin ;
To confess we were wrong, an' are sorry ;
    That loyalty was a sin !

"Ef comin' back they'd been decent,
    Hadn't sneered over Lincoln's grave,
Had left off braggin' uv treason
    An' the cause they couldn't save,
I'd 'ave swallered all resentment
    In spite uv this wooden leg ;
An' ez fer goin' ag'in 'em
    I wouldn't have moved a peg.

" I was ready to bury the hatchet,
    To forgive an' try to forget ;
But beggin Jeff Davis's pardon
    Is ruther the wust thing yet !
The centennial plan of ' oblivion '
    Was good, so fur ez it went, —
To bottle well up our anger,
    But to give to their venom vent !"

The Corporal's Northern blood was up,
    As he muttered, and hobbled away,

From the look and tone he carried,
   I reckon it wasn't to pray.
At every step his wooden stump
   Came down with a vicious vim ;
And it is my calm opinion
   They get no help from him.

He sees an insolent menace
   In the venom of Hill's tirade,
The germ of another secession,
   The stuff of which rebels are made.
But you can depend upon it,
   Whether with ballot or blade,
Enough, upon call, will rally
   To wipe out Hill's Brigade.

MARCH, 1876.

———o○;○;○○———

RE-FORM AT HAMBURG.

"Re-form — without masks — at Hamburg !
   On a white line campaign plan !
An' 'Sun-set' in Congress excuses
   Ez quick ez ever he can ;
Jest like my dog Bose ther',
   Who runs afore I say sic !
Good fellow ! Northern doughface,
   The blood from their hands to lick.

"An' that rebel rag in Missouri,
   Floatin' over a court-house ther' !
With judge, 'n' lawyers, 'n' jury,
   A yellin' *Re-form* in the air !

Re-form! yes, the old line is re-formin
    Wherever they safely can,
To shoot down the colored voters, —
    Centennial campaign plan !

" Then ther's that rag-baby to swoller,
    An' lock-step with Morrissey John,
An' along with old Tammany holler
    Hooray for *Reform!* and move on
The enemy's works, — which is niggers, —
    And down with their friends to a man,
Is what *seems*, at present. the secret
    Confident campaign plan !

" Their blood was ez red ez Custer's,
    An' they're dead sure in the right —
Shot down *after* surrender,
    Not in a stand-up fight,
By them as had no right to do it,
    Hadn't no shadder of excuse
To ask their arms, or receive 'em !
    Why, it's wus'n the bloody Sioux!

" Is *this* their Southern chiv'lry ?
    Is this their kind uv reform ?
It's ruther their criminal deviltry,
    Too fur gone to reform !
It's the same old slave-drivin' devil
    We thought we had cast out an' killed,
When they gave the white flag to Custer,
    'N' we thought enuff blood was spilled.

" When he took that flag at Farmville,
    An' they piled their rusty guns,
We called it Southern manhood,
    Proud uv our nation's sons !
But ef *this* is Southern manhood,
    Their boasted chivalry, too,

Ef this is valor and honor, —
   Wal, — *then the war aint thru!*"

The Corporal turned to his mowing
   In the sweltering July sun, —
A broad clean swarth he was mowing,
   In the meadow along the run ;
. And at every swing of his long, keen blade
   His lips were more firmly set ;
With a muttered curse on the Hamburg raid,
   " They're all blanked rebels yet ! "

And when there is call for soldiers,
   In the coming November storm,
He will be sure to rally,
   The true blue line to re-form, —
And his old wooden leg go stumping,
   I reckon the very first one,
To vote on this Hamburg matter,
   As he voted before with his gun.

JULY 17, 1876.

A SOLID SOUTH.

" So the South is goin' in solid !
   Who can say when it wa'n't ?
What it meant before to be solid,
   Some uv us haint forgot.
They were solid for Jeff and secession,
   An' solid ag'in the flag ;
An' solid in fightin' an' yellin'
   For that Southern bastard rag.

" But ef I remember correctly,
    There was somethin' else solid then,
Which seems, ez now I think uv it,
    Like a line uv blue-bloused men.
An' our batteries blazed an' thundered
    Only one answer forth;
While the old flag floated to emblem
    The will uv a solid North.

" An' ef they are comin 'together,
    Solid an' savage ag'in,
It's only because they're hopin'
    State rights an' Secession will win!
Solid?   Aint rogues alwus solid,
    When the sheriff is on their track
To arrest an' bring 'em to justice,
    An' bring the plunder back?

" An' ez *good* men go in together
    To hunt out a thievin' pack
With no lack uv motives to move 'em,
    No longer slow nor slack,
You'll find the Solid South boastin',
    Brings only one answer forth —
They'll meet, as they met before,
    The ranks of a Solid North."

With whatever lack of honor
    Political leaders stand,
Or lack of unselfish devotion
    To justice and native land,
The Corporal's honor fails not;
    His heart is untarnished and pure;
In his face glows the solemn purpose,
    That the Union shall endure.

God bless the old Corporal's valor,
    His keen and unerring scent,

That this Solid South boast and business
Means what it always meant;
And grant to thwart and defeat them,
To trouble and prosper them not,
That the roused Solid North give answer,
Like the plunge of a solid shot.

Oct., 1876.

--- ∘∘:∘:∘∘ ---

AFTER ELECTION.

" Well, I reckon God isn't cornered,
Nor his light gettin' dim,
That we've got to cheat in the corner,
To carry a point for him!
Yes, God, with one hundred eighty,
Is a surer way to thrive
Than to stain even one uv the figures
That make up eighty-five.

" It's a time uv danger, parson,
For our good old ship of state,
An' the best thing I can think uv
Is jist to quietly wait.
Ef we *must*, why, *yield* the advantage,
Gained by those bulldozin' frauds;
An' then, in the next election,
Roll up the honest odds.

" An' I shall be loyal, parson,
Whichever way it goes;
I'm not the stuff for a rebel,
Though it's ruther a tough old dose;
But we can't allow them canvassers
To stretch a point for us;

Ef they do, the next election
  Will be goin' ag'in us, wus.

"To win is alwus welcome,
  But it's better far to be right;
Especially ef it happens
  That we should have to fight; —
To fight a fraud is fur better
  For the stomach uv a man
Than to go to fightin' *for* 'one, —
  I doubt ef a good man can.

"The old ship seems to be driftin'
  Right onto a rugged rock;
An' I sometimes ruther question
  Ef she can stand the shock.
But we'll man her like men, and stand ready,
  Honest an' square at our post;
An' hope that the silent Captain
  Will find a pass in the coast,

"An' steer the old ship through it,
  Escapin' the rocky bar;
I reckon he haint lost the bearin'
  Uv Truth fur a steerin' star.
It's better to build on jestice;
  It won't do to wink at *wrong;*
Ef God has an eye to this business,
  That can't triumph long.

"I've got more faith in the people —
  The real people, North and South —
Than I have in the brag and bluster
  Uv the hottest fire-eatin' mouth.
An' Fate, with God, will see to it,
  Will smite every infamous fraud,
Till, sooner or later, they'll learn it, —
  They can't steal a march on God.

"So, I reckon God isn't cornered,
  Nor his light gettin' dim,
That we've got to cheat in the shadow,
  To make a point for him.
Whoever goes out in countin',
  Be sure that you count God in,
For it's sure defeat without him,
  Though fur a time you win."

The Corporal touches his old cloth cap
  With the soldier's firm salute,
And stumps with his wooden leg, sturdily,
  Along his daily route.
And in the old fellow's rough horse sense
  There shines a gleam of light
That makes success fade out and pale
  Before the Immortal — Right.

Nov. 27, 1876.

SAUCE FOR THE GANDER.

"Hold up, parson, I tell ye
  It aint no sort uv use
To slap and bang about *Conover!*
  This well-baked Policy goose
Must be carved and served, I reckon.
  Let Thurman cut an' slash;
Let Conover vote for Hamburg, —
  He's legitimate Policy Hash.

"If the noble Hampton's governor now,
  It seems to my limited view
That a *legal* Legislature
  Makes a legal Senator, too.

There's no sort uv use in kickin'
  Ag'in them political pricks;
They're fools, ef with all their schoolin'
  They haven't learned the tricks.

"It's no time *now* to cry baby,
  To mourn they've lost the game;
You can't depend on the swimin'
  Of the duck who wades in lame.
The gong for the feast has sounded,
  An' it aint no sort uv use
To refuse the roast we furnished 'em, —
  They've cooked and 'll carve that goose.

"Then they'll jest pay for it in silver,
  That's legal (an' tender too),
And ef Jonathan should refuse it,
  Then, pray, what can he do?
For he'll lose his goose, an' his Senate
  (Ef the Whigs don't rise to view);
Ef he will not take their silver,
  Then, pray, what can he do?

"Fur Banning 'll make a gesture,
  An' Bland will be child-like an' blue,
While Ewing will soak his little sponge
  In the Ohio (Kentucky, too),
To wipe out our Butler's bloated bonds
  While he watches his pile uv bricks;
And Schurz endangers his elegant limbs
  A-kickin' political pricks!"

Mr. President, Senators, Gentlemen!
  There are men, and not a few,
Who in ways and walks that are humble,
  Keep the Capitol well in view.
Their judgment is not hasty,
  Their aims and their hearts are large;

And they will call you to strict account
   For the trust you took in charge.

The past they have not forgotten,
   Nor the future lost from view :
Though Senates and Presidents pass away,
   The people will yet stand true.
They will render work that is foolish,
   And only the Right shall stand,
For they will smite, stamp out, and slay
   Each trading political band.

HOW THEY CARED FOR JIM.

" It aint very often, parson,
   That I am tempted to swear,
But there's some things so mean 'n' ungrateful,
   So niggardly base 'n' unfair,
That there aint no way uv expressin'
   The rage that is soaked in chagrin
In language that's right 'n' proper, —
   That's when I'm tempted to sin.

" They've sent poor Jim to the almshouse !
   The squire an' the selick men
(Who grew rich ez substitute brokers)
   Got tired uv givin', an' then
They histed him off ez a pauper.
   They're done wastin' money on him,
For all that they promised his father
   That they would look out for Jim.

" Jim's father, at Cedar Mountain,
   Was among the first to fall,

An' when he lay a-dyin'
   All torn by a cannon-ball ;
When strength an' breath was failin'
   An' his eyes a-growin' dim,
He said, 'Tell the squire an' selick men
   To take good care uv Jim.'

"They had all uv his pay an' bounty,
   A-keepin' it snug an' trim,
In case he was killed or disabled,
   To feed an' care for Jim.
You know how they boosted an' farmed him out
   To pay for his board in chores,
Never once gettin' to decent feed
   Nor darkenin' decent doors.

"An' the new selick men have forgotten
   That ever there was a war —
An' the men who died so long ago —
   An' what they all died for ;
So, eager for pacification,
   A-hidin' the bloody past,
They've shipped Jim off to the poor-house,
   An' they're at peace at last.

"Well, I guess we aint a Nation —
   At least worth dyin' for !
Could I safely float the stars an' stripes
   Where I followed them in the war?
They ought to protect a citizen
   In Hamburg or Mobile
Without his havin' a single fear
   Of treacherous lead an' steel.

"But no — the Government has no power
   Till some great Hampton calls,
To protect the life uv its citizens
   From murderous rifle-balls.

What wonder when this doctrine
  Is heard from executive halls,
That the cripple child uv a soldier
  Away to the poor-house crawls?

"We fought for the Union an' saved it —
  We saved it ez we ought;
We fought for the ballot an' lost it,
  An' lost just where we fought,
Unless we vote ez the Southern grays
  A-swaggerin' swear we ought.
No! that aint the Union
  That lived in our loyal thought."

You may doff your hats to Treason,
  The Corporal's conscience yet
Is too keen and sharply consistent
  To allow him to forget;
And thousands of us are with him,
  And glad I surely am
Not to look yet upon loyalty
  As a sentimental sham.

The right to-day is as sacred
  As when, under Southern Stars,
We gathered in line against the lie
  Of rebel Stars and Bars.
If right looms up to-day in the haze
  It is clear we were all wrong then,
And if so there is not a Corporal's guard
  Who would fight for the Union again.

And when the old question confronts us,
  As meet us again it will,
With what heart could loyal legions
  Follow the old cause still?
If they fall, why off to the poor-house
  Their children and wives may go,

And the heart of their cause be clean-cut out
   And thrown to a beaten foe.

We ask of them surely nothing
   But what we readily grant,—
The right of free speech and ballot;
   To reap as well as to plant.
Until these things are free and fair,
   Under Southern as Northern sun,
The work in which our brothers fell
   Cannot be said to be done.

———oo:o:oo———

CLAY IN THE HANDS OF THE PLOTTER.

Ez clay in the hands uv the Potter!
   Well, the old wheel goes 'round,
The Potter obeying the Plotter,
   Who scents all frauds like a hound.
With what acute precision
   He scents a Republican trail,
An' lifts his nose high into the air
   With regulation wail.

How they lift their eyebrows in horror!
   While tongues are thrust into their cheeks,
A-showin' the patriot purpose
   Which "Fraud" & Co. seeks.
They won't ketch the wrong fish this time,
   They don't fish the Tilden pond;
They're only goin' a-fishing,
   Not thinkin' uv what is beyond.

The old Fraud goes a-fraudin';
   He knows how it is himself,

A-smilin' 'an blinkin' so artful,
 The old " cold clam on the shelf."
An' he sings 'an hums, while watchin'
 The mischief he's trying to brew —
Florida and Louisiana —
 Anything more won't do.

They're clay in the hands uv my Potter,
 An' Potter himself is clay ;
Ef the old wheel keeps a-whirlin'
 They'll fall into line 'an obey.
Can't I scent a fraud and find it?
 I'm breathin' my native air ; —
Just skip New York an' Oregon,
 For Goff and Cypher are there !

About *those* frauds no matter ;
 I've seen all them before ;
We want only a trail to take us
 Right up to the White House door ;
An' then we'll walk up boldly
 (We didn't mean it before),
An' Rutherford? — oh ! he'll meekly
 Back out uv some back door.

The old "cold clam " is a-warmin'
 A horrible, terrible stew :
Why, he'd cut up even the White House !
 It'll make fine kindlin', too, —
This fine old Railroad Wrecker,
 A-waitin' to clutch the spoils,
No matter what goes for kindlin' .
 Ef his own fraud pot-boils.

WANTED: A CAPTAIN.

Ef God's everlastin' purposes
   Concernin' this favored land
Depend on sich tools ez Anderson
   An' the cards in Tilden's hand,
I reckon he'd throw up the business,
   Just close the old thing out ; —
But I reckon his purpose is deeper,
   An' he will bring it about.

I can't think he is planin'
   To let the whole thing slip ;
I reckon he'll find a master
   To sail the good old ship.
He's got too much invested,
   Too much by far at stake,
To allow his plans to miscarry
   By any one man's mistake.

I don't fear for the safety
   Uv the cargo, nor the ship,
Because God's cables an' anchors
   Are not very likely to slip.
He rules the tides an' the currents,
   The calms an' eddys, all ; —
An' the good old ship won't founder
   In any sudden squall.

An' he will "lay to" to help us,
   Sendin' a Pilot aboard !
With God for convoy an' escort
   To wait we can well afford.
So we'll throw the anchor uv *jestice*
   Held well by cables uv law ;
Clew up our sail, an' safely
   Ride out the sudden flaw.

With colors at peak an' mizzen,
   Nailed up sure an' fast,
Though the white squall whirl an' whistle,
   Its fury will soon be past.
An' when once more on the quarter-deck
   We hear the old Captain's tread,
An' hear his trumpet a-callin'
   "Stand by, to heave the lead!"

"Shake out the main-sail uv labor;
   Look sharp! stand by to belay!"
He'll put about on the right course,
   An' we shall be under way.
Then we shall gather headway,
   An' then the old sails will fill,
An' belly an' tug an' take us away,
   Obeyin' the Captain's will.

All that we want is a Captain;
   So we'll anchor an' ride the gale,
Till the old Tanner's gig uv leather
   Heaves to alongside to hail.
An' then we'll man the old gangway,
   Throw the old rope-ladder out,
Welcoming home from foreign shore
   With tremendous cheer an' shout.

An' then the whole gang uv traitors
   Who are tryin' to scuttle the ship
Shall be ironed by public opinion,
   Chained by a righteous grip.
An' cargo, an' crew, an' passengers,
   Shall lose all cause uv fear,
"Steady," shall be the word at the wheel;
   "Aye, aye, sir," the answer clear.

THE CORPORAL BREAKS SILENCE.

"I've been tryin', parson,
　　To find where I am, an' what:
That I *was* a Union soldier
　　I hardly have forgot,
But *why* I was, or the good uv it,
　　Don't seem plain to-day;
That I'd go again, if able,
　　I'm not quite ready to say.

"They've thrown away the victory
　　We bought with toil an' blood;
Hear the Senate and House a-ringin'
　　With roar uv treason's flood;
The crew a-conspirin' to scuttle
　　The good old Union ship!
Ef the man at the wheel don't save us,
　　They've got us in their grip.

"An' they'll jest ez surely triumph
　　Ez we allow them to gain
Control uv the helm an' keep it;
　　The plan uv their fight is ez plain
Ez ever their line of battle,
　　When in more manly way
They sought to wrest a victory
　　From the heat uv deadly fray.

"My hope is that the reptile
　　Whose rattle an' venomous hiss
Gave us of old, sure warning,
　　Will rattle again in this
His renewed an' reckless battle,
　　Agin Union with the North;
Ef so, we may know the course
　　On which his hate goes forth.

"The fang uv that snake is deadly.
     Let us hope that his rattle is sure ;
That he won't have the sense to hide it,
     While we're asleep secure,
But on the floor of the Senate,
     An' in the lower hall,
Will unwittingly sound the summons
     That again to the lines will call,

"All who fought for the Union,
     All who gave brothers an' friends,
To rally again to meet them,
     Though the Solid South defends.
Where is the faith an' the spirit,
     That arose in 'sixty-one,
Standin' unflinchin' an' loyal,
     Until the battle was done ?

"Let us leave our soldiers' monuments,
     An' level their humble graves ;
Hide our old swords an' muskets,
     An' cringe like a pack uv slaves
Before the swagger an' flourish ;
     No, ' we've come back to stay '
An' suck the blood uv the nation,
     An' *vote* its life away !

"Ef my old leg in the Wilderness
     Doesn't kick their traitorous sod,
I swear I will not own it
     In the last great day uv God,
When he in the resurrection
     Gives back my buried limb ;
 I'll limp forever through glory, —
     Ef it's all the same to him,

" Before I'll wear about me
     One bit uv blood or bone

That doesn't hate treason forever,
 Whether its front is shown
On the lines of the Appomattox,
 Or in legislative halls;
Whether it fight with bullets,
 Or slay with ballot balls."

Four years since the Corporal
 · Predicted Hill's Brigade
Would make on the Union Congress
 A fatal and deadly raid.
He has lived to see Hill in the Senate,
 And to hear a live rebel say,
" We're here to sweep every vestige
 Of war legislation away."

FALL IN !

[Written for the " Bangor Daily Whig and Courier," and published within a few days of the State Election, held in Maine, Sept. 8, 1879, and the last of the Political Series of the Old Corporal Ballads, and the last but one of Mr. Coan's satires.]

We're formin' the old line, comrades,
 In our good old Pine Tree State,
Uv the men who were boys in 'fifty-six,
 An' in 'sixty voted straight
For the sainted Abraham Lincoln,
 With a purpose plain an' clear,
That swept to the goal uv victory
 With loyal an' ringin' cheer.

Last year there was dissatisfaction;
 Deserters were all along,
Who wouldn't close in with the column,
 But swelled the stragglers' throng,

That lost us the State an' the battle
  Which by right we should have won,
An' *would*, ef we'd wisely measured
  The work that was bein' done.

We were sold to the foe we had battled,
  Yes, whipt, without favor or fear ;
A foe we can always handle
  Ef the issue is plain an' clear.
An' now that we've heard the warnin'
  Uv venomous rattle an' hiss,
We propose to write on our banners
  A victory in this,

Our campaign for honest money,
  For honest an' loyal men ; —
For freedom, an' right uv ballot,
  Anywhere, an' anywhere.
For, ef they can Yazoo Dimercrats,
  On the Mississippi plan,
They are really robbin' the franchise
  Uv every Northern man.

For each one they slay, or frighten
  Away from a freeman's right,
In Yazoo, Memphis, or Hamburg,
  It's the same ez ef shot in our sight :
It is freedom that they are slayin'
  With assassin's shot an' stab,
However Lamar an' the leaders
  May whine out their loyal gab.

The cloven foot uv their purpose
  Is too soon an' too plainly shown
To the men who have faced their rifles
  An' the sound uv their yell have known.
So three times three an' a tiger,
  Shall rend our September air

Till *their* famished an' hungry tiger
    Skulks away to his hidden lair.

So here's to our Corporal Davis
    Who shall grace our Governor's chair;
Honest men an' honest money,
    With elections on the square,
An' the Greenback-Grayback alliance,
    A delusion all an' a snare,
Shall show up the Salt river rapids
    To camp on the head-waters there!

It's a rill to which they're accustomed,
    They know the spot uv their camp,
Although last year they wandered
    From the beat uv their usual tramp.
Already their scouts are explorin'
    A suitable campin' place,
For they scent defeat in the air,
    An' know they have lost the race.

THE PARSON TO THE CORPORAL.

They might hope to harness the whirlwind;
    They might hope to check the tide;
But had better not make the endeavor
    To stem the current and ride
On an angry public upheaval,
    Thinking to make it go
Some other way than the fated
    Course of its certain flow.

When rebels stand up to berate us
    For our part in 'sixty-one,

It seems that Pacification's
  Work is clumsily done!
The cloven foot of their motive
  Appears a little too quick
To leave them a chance of succeeding
  In the work of their treacherous trick.

If you give enough rope to the devil
  He is sure to hang himself!
The doughface politician is sure to find his place,
  Is sure to find his shelf,
And climb to it briskly,
  And pack himself away,
As ever the night is sure
  To follow the light of day.

Let them howl on, then, and threaten!
  They only make more sure
The fate we have predicted, —
  That men will not endure
Their rashly renewed endeavor
  To do through political strife
What they failed to do before
  With bullet and bowie-knife.

So look sharp to their Congress;
  Be ready and quick to hear
The yell of those rampant rebels;
  So rang their joyful cheer
When the lines of the loyal faltered,
  Or turned white faces to God;
When their red blood flowing freely
  Enriched their Southern sod.

We forget not the foes who fought us
  So long as *that* old-time cheer
From the ranks of political leaders
  In Congress we plainly hear.

But stand alert, and ready
  To strike for freedom and right,
Whether with arms they front us
  Or in political ambush fight.

———oo°o°oo———

THE OLD BUGLE CALL.

Bring out the old battered bugle
  That sounded in 'sixty-one,
Rousing each gray-headed father,
  Daughter, and daring son.
We have not all forgotten
  Those stirring heroic days
When the fairest for the bravest
  Twined their immortal bays.

It is well that some of us see clearly
  The drift of commercial stream,
And dare on the tide swift rushing
  The light of truth to beam;
And to swear in the light of those lessons,
  And the lost light of loyal eyes,
To kindle anew the signals
  That shall flash athwart the skies.

The lessons of the brave dead teach us,
  As though they were with us yet;
The look of whose eyes as we closed them
  We never can forget,
When they lay in the damps of evening,
  After the battle was done,
Pulseless, cold, and livid,
  Cold, under tropic sun.

We forgive the brave who fought us,
    Nor cling to one thought of war ;
But will hate forever and deeply
    The *cause* which they suffered for ;
And will hate it and fight it forever,
    And them, if they dare defend
The fratricide right of secession,
    Which we thought the war would end.

We have guns yet, swords, and saddles,
    That are red with loyal stains,
Hid now under rust which encrusts them
    With each year's suns and rains ;
And until Time's hand efface them,
    Those tokens of loyal death,
We swear that our hearts shall be loyal
    And our lives breathe loyal breath.

And whatever guise that serpent
    State Sovereignty shall wear,
We will tear off that guise, and throttle
    Till its heart from its carcass we tear ;
For we learned to hate treason and traitors,
    And will teach to our daughters and sons
The lessons from lips and faces
    Made livid by State Sovereign guns.

THE SAME OLD FLAG.

Bring out the old campaign colors,
   Hoist the old banner high,
With starry blue and crimson,
   Clear in the autumn sky, —
The same old flag that in 'sixty,
   And later in 'sixty-one,
We hailed with tears of devotion,
   When the skies were heavy and dim.

We followed it in its peril,
   That its folds might know no stain ;
And now that dishonor threatens
   We rally around it again.
We perilled our lives for its honor ;
   Can we not give watchful toil,
That no fanatic delusion
   Its unsullied lustre soil?

When the old world's socialist convicts
   Hiss out fanatic hate,
Assailing our free republic
   As they would a tyrannous state,
We will rally around the standard,
   We will lift the old banner high,
Will vote and toil for its honor,
   As once we were ready to die.

Defending now with the ballot,
   As we did with the bayonet then,
With cordons of steel and iron,
   In the hands and hearts of men,
We will give no vote to dishonor
   The sheen of its starry flow,
That shall shame when in the future
   The deeds of to-day are told.

We fought disunion and treason
   As loyal freemen then ;
And now dishonor and folly
   In the hearts of misguided men.
Though the load to be borne is heavier
   Than we in the darkness saw,
We may not refuse without breaking
   The sacred ægis of law.

'Tis the fate of war and the nation,
   Cursed by a traitor's crew ;
Though they were false to their pledges,
   For us it remained to be true.
We stand by the bond — our honor
   And safety bind us there ;
Of breaking the nation's pledges
   It behooves us well to beware.

BANGOR, Sept. 9, 1880.

PART II.

PART II.

---oo:̌o:̌oo---

SIMON GAREW.

A LEGEND OF GULF GLEN.*

If I could paint the North Maine woods,
 The sweep of grand old hills,
The bald gray granite mountain range,
 The clear moss-bedded rills ;
Bring scent of balsam odors here,
 Or sounds of forest night,
The soughing wind in tasselled pine,
 The glow of camp-fire light ;
Or etch the flash of speckled trout
 Through deep, clear mountain pool ;
Or sketch September sunsets, and
 The night air clear and cool ;
The relished fare, the hunger keen,
 The game-feast spread in camp ;
Or slumber deep on scented boughs
 After a day's long tramp,—

Sketch you the fair Ebemee *
 As pleasant as it sounds,
Or give the rugged Hagus Gorge ;*
 The mountain, hunting-grounds ;
The graceful poise of startled deer,
 The rough, majestic moose,

---

* See note at end of book.

The swift, ungraceful caribou,
　　The wily hunter's ruse ; —
I then would paint exactly where
　　The old guide sat and told
Of strange Garew, the French half-breed,
　　And frontier days of old, —
Would paint the jutting boulders there,
　　The strong human face,
So silent, thoughtful, stern and grand,
　　That you might know the place
Where still it hangs, the same as then,
　　On rugged mountain side,
Gazing adown the wild old glen
　　Into the torrent's tide.

Nor pen nor pencil reproduce
　　Such scenes and sounds as those,
The best eludes the artist's skill
　　As odor in the rose.
So only now the story weird
　　Of old-time frontier day,
Repeating here the old guide's words,
　　As near as ballad may : —

＊　　＊　　＊　　＊　　＊　　＊　　＊

"Have a light?　There ! that is better.
　　How's this for a camping-place?
You'll have to move back to the shelter,
　　Or the heat will scorch yer face.
Never heard of Garew?　That's queer.
　　'Twas 'round Ebemee, and here
He came with his dog and rifle, —
　　Came twice in every year.

"Once when the snow was crusted,
　　And once when the leaves were red,
And the river was low in Hagus,
　　So he could follow the bed ;

His mother, an Oldtown Indian girl,
  By a roving French trader betrayed;
But a noiseless Indian arrow
  Avenged the beautiful maid.

" But the child grew silent and thoughtful,
  And always every year,
After he grew to manhood,
  Came twice to this forest here.
Still he lived with his mother at Oldtown;
  And when, at last, she died,
He followed alone to her burial
  With only his dog at his side.

" And still he kept the old cabin,
  With the same half-savage ways,
Till he grew to be old and feeble
  In his own last, lonely days;
And then all the neighbors wondered
  What made him persist to go
To the Gulf when the leaves grew red,
  And again on the crusted snow.

" But at last he told them his secret,
  With great solemnity said : —
' The Great Spirit comes to the face in the rock,
  The moon when the leaves grow red;
And when the round moon shines upon it,
  Shines into the Gulf at night,
Shines full and fair upon it,
  Making it plain and white, —

" ' Whoever waits there, with fasting,
  Below the strong face,
With a young deer's blood for offering,
  Always finds pardon and peace.'

This the Great Spirit had told him,
   And had many times proved true ;
And once more he purposed going,
   Though he solemnly said he knew

" (The Great Spirit surely had told him)
   He would never again come out ;
Yet still would he go and die there
   (Of this he had never a doubt).
So soon as the August moon told him
   The waters in Hagus were low,
To be sure of the needed offering,
   With rifle and dog would go.

" He went, as purposed, and living
   He came not out again,
And the villagers down the river
   Watched for his coming in vain.
That time the face of the full moon
   Shone not on the face in the rock,
For a storm hung black in the heavens,
   And the winds and the tempest's shock

" Roared through a week of storms,
   Such as ever and only is known
When the storm is too dense and heavy
   To be lifted by the moon.
That autumn, they say, the hunters
   Saw lingering in the glen
A strange dog, gaunt and wistful,
   Going and coming again

" To the point whence we see the face ;
   And the legend also saith
That the faithful dog, like his master,
   Was faithful unto death.

Near the close of that week of tempests
  The full moon's night came on,
But the storm hung heavy and sullen,
  The stars and the moon were gone.

" Gray and turgid the river rose,
  And roared down the fearful glen,
And just at his time of offering, —
  The storm was wildest then, —
Did he wait there alone in the darkness,
  Watching in vain for the face?
Did he perish in the floods that
  Roar down that fearful place?

" Well, the Indians down the river,
  And some other people, say,
That still on the moon when the leaves are red,
  The very same hour of the day
When the full moon shines into Hagus,
  The man and the dog come back
And wait for the pardon he found not,
  The night when the storm was black."

        *   *   *   *   *

If now the light of weird camp-fire,
  The old guide's dreamy maze,
Could flash and gleam a moment here;
  The flickering, fitful blaze
Shine here upon you as you read,
  And darkness gathers round;
The river's ceaseless monotone;
  The night birds in the tree;
The beast's wild yell in forest near
  That seems your blood would freeze,
And you could lend your fancy
  To the leadings of all these;
Could drift and dream along the maze
  Of stray and sombre spell

To which my vagrant fancies then,
    After listening, fell,—
Then I might hope this border tale
    Might seem the same to you
As there that night it seemed to me, —
    This Legend of Garew.

TRIBUTE OF SMILES AND TEARS.

A JUNE SONG.

Bobolink, jaunty and joyous !
    Brave singer, I greet you to-day !
Would I could weave your music
    And melody into my lay.
Could I catch its rollicking movements,
    Its melody, liquid and clear,
Its generous, wild abandon,
    Its gladsome, challenging cheer ;

Its joy of anticipation,
    Its love of mate and young,
I would fill the air with the sweetest
    Song that ever was sung ;
Pour it out with ecstatic pleasure
    On the tremulous, throbbing air,
Filling men's hearts with its solace
    For toil and worry and care.

I would strive to sing away sadness
    From the hearts of sorrowing men,
Until they should listen and love me,
    And bless me again and again,

As I have blessed you for your riotous,
  Rapturous rush of song,
Until heart after heart should echo
  Your generous strain, and prolong.

O bird of my boyhood's fancy !
  Do you know how you bring back the years
Before life was earnest and tragic,
  Or my eyes had been dim with tears
For the dead and the dying,
  Or my heart had been torn with pain,
Or become the place of burial
  For bright hopes ruthlessly slain?

My mother's kind voice, and the loving,
  Radiant light of her face,
Making home bright by its presence
  With nameless and blessèd grace ;
Sweet sisters, brothers and playmates, .
  Father and questioning boy, —
All come thronging around me
  Through the rush of your turbulent joy.

Sing, brave bird of June joy,
  Heed not my pleasure or tears !
How little you know that you people
  The air with life of those years,
Some of them gleaming with sabres,
  Red with the blood of the slain,
Which come trooping back at your summons, -
  Your song has not been in vain.

And white faces that are reposing,
  With pale hands folded and crossed,
In silence sweep past my vision,
  While the trill of your song has been tossed
With such defiant abandon
  Out over the roses of June,

In strange and curious contrast
   To the roll of your jubilant tune.

So into my heart the minor
   Refrain of memory came,
Unbidden, but blessed and welcome ;
   And you the power may claim,
From the spell of your magical genius,
   On through Time's coming years,
What I your song have rendered,
   A tribute of smiles and tears.

SOLOMON SHIRK.

Old Solomon Shirk was a blue hard-shell,
   With a hatchet face, and a long hooked nose ;
We all knew the tale he used to tell
   When he in prayer-meeting arose.
He was such a sinner ! you wouldn't believe
   If he was telling about it.
Yet it came with an unction you cannot conceive,
   And some of us didn't doubt it.

But he did not mean it any while,
   And if another had said it
Would have put on his resignation smile,
   Giving persecution credit ;
A poor, sick neighbor might starve and die, —
   He would not bother about it ;
And this was just the reason why
   Some of us didn't doubt it.

The generous Master's golden rule
  To him was a meaningless myth ;
And in life's rough-and-tumble school
  He knew neither kin nor kith ;
The years did not mellow his leathern heart,
  Nor abate his clutch of pelf ;
In Charity's mission he had no part,
  He loved alone his own mean self.

In an old red school-house a meeting was held ;
  It was full, " the interest intense ; "
At the usual time the crowd beheld
  " Old Sol " arise ; a pause, — suspense.
But he told the worn and hackneyed tale,
  Of his fearful, " terrible, wicked heart,"
And closing with his old lugubrious wail,
  Sat down, having " taken a part."

Then up rose Jim, a *sinner* indeed, —
  Of *this* we hadn't a doubt.
When he arose they all gave heed,
  For " Jim must be a-comin' out."
" What that mean old hulk is sayin' is true,
  And I can bear witness tew it ;
Ef there's anything meaner'n the devil can dew,
  He is jist the sinner to dew it."

SKATING SONG.

The bright steel rings ; the skater swings
   With rhythmic movement, lithe and slow,
To deftly glide o'er the frozen tide,
   While fair cheeks flush with mantling glow.
The ice-field rings ; like flash of wings
   The cloud of fleet forms flying fast,
With swifter rush and deafening flush ;
   The sport of winter reigns at last.

With graceful whirl and gleaming swirl
   They spin with deft and swift device ;
And cut the name of blushing fame
   In feathery monogram of ice.
Away, away ! they rush away,
   O'er gleaming lake and crystal bay ;
Nor bird on wing nor flying thing
   Can whirl with swifter grace than they !

Like maze of dance, or flying lance,
   A tournament of sport and glee ;
Nor would refuse to sing the muse
   Of olden sports and minstrelsy.
The strain prolong, ye joyous throng !
   Shout out your songs on winter air ;
Nor pine for ways of other days,
   For youth more lithe nor maids more fair.

So now we slide with homeward glide,
   The north wind whirls us down the bay ;
Nor ease nor pride shall set aside
   This splendid sport of winter's day.
The bright steel rings ; the skater swings
   With rhythmic movement, lithe and slow ;
They fleetly glide o'er frozen tide,
   While fair cheeks flush with mantling glow.

DECEMBER, 1876.

IN AFFLICTION.

Alike over sunshine and darkness
  Bendeth the heaven of God,
We stumble and bleed in the pathway
  Where thousands before have trod, —
Have trod with grief as bitter,
  With struggles as blind and wild,
And passed on into the sunshine
  Where Heaven again had smiled.

Though the stars are hidden in darkness,
  Though the light of day depart,
Light above abides unchanging,
  Though hidden from eye and heart.
Hold still! in the fire of the furnace,
  Yea, have you not been told,
From heat that is white and blinding
  Gleameth out the moulten gold?

JANUARY 18, 1878.

WATER LILIES.

Our little white lily has fallen;
  It dropped on a barren strand,
And floated away on the water,
  Beyond the reach of my hand.

Into the mists and the darkness,
  Far away from the clamorous strife,
It floats, and I may not reach it, —
  My little white lily of life.

Oh, the little white face of my darling !
  How it shone with a light serene,
As cleaving the turbulent river,
  Its tremulous light was seen !

And now the mists rise in the darkness,
  And the black spray dashes afar,
But flashing and white in the distance
  That little face shines as a star.

Though the waves of that river are fearful,
  And the storm on its bosom is wild,
There is floating, untouched by terror,
  The face of a little child.

———o·:·o·:·o———

THE ROBINS' CALL.

All through the beautiful summer, —
  The last that our darling was here, —
The robins sang out so sweetly,
Speaking so plainly and neatly
  Their meaning was always clear,
To the golden head that kept dancing
  In and out the long day through,
Flitting like one of their number,
With no fear or care to encumber
  The joy his blithe heart knew.

I am sure they knew and called him,
  Well aware of his prattle and play ;
When he strolled to the tree where they nested,
Unruffled they worked on, or rested, —
  No fear of our darling had they.

And when the brown autumn had silenced
  The noise of their turbulent song,
They seemed saddened at thought of leaving
Our darling alone to be grieving
  For them the whole winter long.

But when the last flock had vanished,
  And fallen the last autumn leaf,
When the bare fields, brown and forsaken,
No more to their echoes awaken,
  Seemingly silent in grief,
Little golden head ceased his flitting
  In and out at the open door, —
Flew away like the birds of the summer,
His trusting playfellows of summer,
  To rest in our arms no more.

When the robins came back to our garden,
  With the early days of spring,
And awoke us from morning slumber,
The sweetest of all their number
  Came close to our window to sing:
"Come out, little golden hair, darling;
  Come out for your morning play;
We are here bright and early to meet you,
With the loudest of songs to greet you,
  The sweetest bright hour of the day!"

And then he waited and listened,
  Then quickly around by the door,
More loudly, sweetly, and purely,
With music of human speech surely,
  Would the same sweet summons outpour.
And all day long he kept calling,
  And still he seemed to say:
"Come out, little golden-haired Freddie,
We're waiting; strange you're not ready;
  You were always ready for play."

And after their nest was finished,
    When, peeping out over the brim,
They seemed to wait for his coming,
They listened, it seemed, for his drumming,
    Mournfully chirping for him ;
And now, every day, they keep calling,
    With a challenge loud and clear ;
Or, pausing, they listen and ponder,
Musing, with bird-like wonder,
    Why golden head does not hear.

FALL RIVER, June, 1874.

CRADLE SONG.

Come, fairy, come, fairy,
    And build me a palace,
A castle, a castle,
    . Hung high in the air ;
Build well for my darling,
    My wee lady Alice,
Build it and fill it
    With radiance rare.
Build that impurity
    Never may mar it ;
Build that the joy of joy
    Ever may cheer it ;
Build that sweet purity ·
    Never may fear it ;
Yes, bathe it and fill it
    With radiance rare.

Singing low lullabies
    To sweet little Alice ;

Singing slow and softly, —
   She floats on the air,
Floating slowly away
   To her dreamland palace,
And fairy-land welcome
   Awaiting her there.
O God! keep my darling,
   My sweet sleeping darling,
My merry-eyed, rosy-lipped,
   Dimpled-touched darling!
Forgive the light fancy
   I sing to my darling,
And fit for thy palace,
   With radiance rare.

WIDE AWAKE.

Dear little clear-eyed Jessie;
   What do you see afar
In the evening's deepening shadows?
   Oh, the Evening Star!
Two eyes wide with wonder,
   Little hands dimpled and pink,
Resting here in the twilight,
   What does my little one think?

Smiling so happy and peaceful,
   Dreamily gazing afar,
The little white face of my darling
   Wondering at a star.
Dreamily droop her eyelids
   Over her limpid eyes,
Swaying here in the twilight
   Sweet little Jessie lies.

Alice, the baby-mother,
  Whispers, while gliding around,
Fearing to wake the sleeper,
  Moving without a sound, —
"Just see my darling sister!
  Isn't she darling, ma?
Gone to sleep in her cradle
  While she was watching a star."

Wide awake, Alice watches;
  She is a "lady" now,
Care for dear little sister
  Marking her baby brow.
But *her* lids drop while watching,
  Dreamily gazing afar,
Joins "dear little sister" sleeping,
  While she is watching a star.

Sleep, sweet babes, in the twilight!
  Lips apart over pearls,
The sweet breath of the sleepers
  Swaying a tangle of curls.
May the dawn of day be sure,
  Sure, but be it far,
When their bright eyes shall awaken
  To the light of the Morning Star.

THE OVERLAND EASTERN.

Rush and rattle ! roar and scream !
Crash through the night like a meteor's gleam !
    Death or life, dashing on !
    Thundering, crashing on !
A glance of a grim Titanic dream !
A flash of the iron-black wing of steam !

Out and on ! and on ! and far away !
Dashing on into the dawn of day !
    Light and shade roaring on !
    Flashing and thundering on !
Shooting into the night a fiery spray !
Careering on over the iron way !

Before it those unwound ribbons of steel
Awaiting the iron coursers heel !
    Waiting the steady, clear
    Glance of the engineer ;
The rhythmic throb of the flying wheel !
The messenger swift of woe and weal !

Behind it the sullenly silent track !
The voiceless night, now silent and black ;
    Like a dream ! like a flash !
    Through a thunderous crash ; —
A far-away warning scream echoing back
Over those lustreless lines of black !

Shivering, pulseless, fateful thing !
Lustreless flash of an iron wing !
    Panting and shrieking !
    Lifeless, yet reeking !
Making the starless welkin ring
With the thunderous storm of sound you bring !

Rush and rattle! roar and scream!
Crash through the night like a meteor's gleam!
　　Death or life, dashing on!
　　Thundering, crashing on! —
The glance of a grim Titanic dream!
A flash of the night-black wing of steam!

——oo◦◦◦oo——

THE MOUNTAIN RILL.

A mountain rill, purling down a glen
　　Among pebbles and green mossy banks,
Quenching thirst of wanderers now and then,
　　Seeing liquid eyes brimming with thanks,

Sighed, "Oh, we go plashing and tumbling down
　　Where multitudes daily meet,
To gladden sad hearts in the sultry town,
　　And freshen the torrid street."

But alas! and alas! the brook knew not
　　Its need of its own green dell;
That it needed the charm of sylvan spot,
　　For the power of its siren spell;

That gutter, or sewer, or putrid drain,
　　Is a rill in the crowded town;
A scouring servant, bound by chain,
　　Despised by the meanest clown;

Or held by the fountain's hand,
　　In art's superb device,
Chained in marble by sylvan band
　　With the chill of imprisoned ice.

O mountain rill ! mountain song flowing free !
　　Despise not thy birthright again,
If throngs do not flock to be soothed by thee,
　　Bless the wanderer now and then.

A PICTURE.

The old First New England Cavalry
　　In line of battle stood,
At the base of a hill * whose rounded top
　·Was crowned with a crest of wood, —
Crowned with a crest of hidden steel
　　And a band † of rebel gray,
While batteries, masked and unmenacing,
　　In treacherous silence lay ;

But "boot and saddle" has sounded,
　　And they must charge the wood
Over that fateful grassy slope —
　　Those strong steeds, stanch and good.
"Charge !" flares the bugle, —
　　And the blue line sweeps away
To where the storm of hurtling lead
　　In waiting silence lay.

The banner, unfurled, flies forward ;
　　The spurs touch bleeding flanks,
While loyal blood is boiling
　　All along the rushing ranks.
Like a living thing that splendid line
　　Sweeps up and up the hill ;
But the wood that crowns the summit
　　Is with boding silence still.

---

*Cedar Mountain.　　　　† "Stonewall's" forces, masked.

A single gun ! a crown of flame
    Encircles the brow of the hill,
And the batteries' hidden menace
    Belches forth its deadly will.
The air is alive with bullets' hiss ; —
    O God, see the blue forms fall !
A moment more of a storm like this
    And the ground must cover all !

No recall sounded the bugle,
    But the rent line wavered, fled,
Tearing over that fateful slope,
    Now covered with dying and dead.
A handful flying headlong down
    Away from the rebel shout ; —
Going in a full battalion,
    But barely a squad came out.

The faithful bugle call rallies them !
    They are forming in line again ;
Here and there horses fly riderless,
    Here and there crouching men.
But see ! down the slope comes tearing, —
    A horseman ? No ! a horse ;
Rushing straight down to the forming line,
    Leaping over the dead in his course.

A lone white horse, with flowing mane
    And nostril distended wide,
His red blood pouring with every leap
    Down over his milk-white side !
He reaches the line, wheels into place,
    Though flows the crimson tide,
Fronting the foe with dauntless face, —
    But an empty saddle must ride.

A moment he stood, and down the line
    A wild thrill slowly crept ;

They brushed the falling tears away,
  Nor blushed they that they wept.
A moment he stood, with head borne high,
  With streaming, tremulous flanks;
Then a shudder ran through his royal frame,
  And he fell and died in the ranks.

It may be treason to tell a tale
  With spirit of deeds like this;
But if we dare not tell them still,
  The dead in their graves will hiss!
With no malice for the living,
  We come with uncovered head,
And swear, while sun and stars shall shine,
  To honor the loyal dead.

----o·o:·o:ov----

THE SOLDIERS' MONUMENT.

[Read at the dedication of the the Soldiers' Monument at Dover, N.H.,
Sept. 14, 1877.]

We were boys when the first gun thundered,
And we waited in fear and wondered,
  With a vague sense of evil to come:
For we knew not the meaning of battle,
We knew not the musketry's rattle,
  Nor the roll of the wakening drum.

But signs of strife gathered round us;
By our books and farms they found us;
  As the sick and the wounded came back,
Bringing fire to young hearts of tinder,
What power on earth could hinder
  A flame springing swift from their track?

Like a dream the old scenes rise before us,
In the blue the old banner floats o'er us;
　　See, the blue line steadily comes!
They are gone, leaving fathers and mothers;
Leaving sisters and wives, and — others,
　　At the call of the bugle and drum.

Through the shadow and shine of autumn suns
The war cloud gathered its blackness dun,
　　And short letters came from the front,
Bringing lists of the dead and the dying,
Who, with heroes of history vying,
　　Went down in the battle's front.

But what pen can picture the gloom of those years:
A nation's agony, blood, and tears,
　　With graves from shore to shore?
The sad voice of fate from executive halls
Trembles with sorrow, but bravely calls
　　For three hundred thousand more!

And never in vain that sad voice calls,
Never in vain his summons falls,
　　From graves with fresh earth covered o'er,
He sees, through eyes that are dim with tears,
The need at the end of three red years,
　　Of three hundred thousand more!

Oh, hang out your banners in peace to-day,
Nor blush to believe, nor fear to say,
　　"The cause was worthy for which they died;"
They were Liberty's sons, and her banner fair
May well float in the blue of our autumn air,
　　To emblem a nation's pride.

You may cover their graves with marble and stone,
And blazon their names from zone to zone, —
　　Unless true to the truth for which they bled

They will bid you blot out each chiselled name,
And blush at the marble lie of fame,
   And rejoice that they sleep with the dead.

Their ensign means justice to one and to all;
If justice fail its folds may fall,
   And for it we shed no tear;
Emblazon it, gild it, bang it high;
Unless justice triumphs it flaunts a lie, —
   Its defenders sleep not here.

Far purer than marble, more lasting than stone,
The monument where their deeds are shown, —
   The temple they proudly reared,
Whose base from the far Pacific shore
To the wild Atlantic's ceaseless roar
   Their dying vision cheered.

Build that, from the lakes to southern sea,
And make it indeed "the home of the free,"
   And then they shall rest in peace,
And smile when marble and granite rise
To pierce the overhanging skies, —
   An emblem of man's release.

You may garnish their graves and thunder with guns,
But if you forget their daughters and sons
   Who suffer as paupers to-day,
You publish your shame, for you told them all,
"We will care for your children if you fall;"
   Believing they went their way.

Believing your promise, they smiled and died
With the soldier's simple faith and pride
   In the home of the noble free;
That their children might safely stand beside
Their graves, and the spot whereon they died,
   Unscathed by "chivalry."

LITTLE BEN.

In sight of old Katahdin
   I sat in a woodman's camp,
In the generous glow of an evening fire, —
   Which was furnace, and even lamp, —
Listening to varied stories,
   Quaintly and aptly told, —
Some of them braggart boasting,
   Others thrilling and bold.

But one was so full of pathos,
   That weird, though mellow spell
On the brawniest boaster in the lot
   In curious contrast fell;
Hushing the tide of that turbulent mirth,
   That boisterous jovial glee; —
And as near as I can, in phrase and words,
   I tell as 'twas told to me:

"Little Ben was the child of a soldier
   Who died in the Union war,
Jest a little before poor Mary,
   Who the angels waited for;
Who, when she lay a-dyin',
   And cryin' for little Ben,
Gave the boy to farmer 'Bijah —
   And the angels took her then.

"Her eyes were large and dreamy,
   The neighbors thought her queer,
And looked with a kind of wonder
   On her face so pale and clear.
Benny was frail and blue-eyed,
   The same light in his eyes,
And he asked such cur'ous questions,
   And made such strange replies.

"'Bijah — he was known for a rough, hard man,
    And never a tender word
To a soul save little baby Bell
    From him was ever heard.
He worked his farm in the summer,
    In the winter, in the woods;
His home was plain and simple,
    And was scant of worldly goods.

" With never a thought of restin',
    Hoardin' and stintin' he saved,
While he and all around him
    Not simply worked, but slaved.
So little Ben grew thinner,
    Wantin' love and over-worked,
While 'Bijah fretted and scolded,
    Thinkin' he always shirked.

" So the reins his rough hands tightened,
    And he sometimes used the rod;
But the blue eyes only brightened,
    Maybe with thinkin' of God.
So, without a single murmur,
    Or rough or hasty way,
He grew paler and weaker and sadder,—
    His little life wastin' away.

" One day in the dead of winter,
    When the man to his work had gone,
When Bell and Benny and Nancy
    Were left at home alone,
That mother's fear fell sudden, —
    The croupy cry they heard, —
And baby Bell was a-stiflin';
    They must send the father word.

" But 'twas miles away and winter,
    While the day was so bitter cold

That scarce could a man in safety
   His way to the deep woods hold.
But baby Bell was a-dyin',
   And while his poor heart bled,
The scant-clothed form of Benny
   Away for 'Bijah sped.

"Bitter and keener blew the wind,
   The cold more fearful grew,
As over the crisp an' frozen snow
   His eager footsteps flew.
But the frost, like Fate, was pitiless,
   For his hands began to freeze;
His feet grew numb an' painless,
   As he faced the icy breeze.

"But he prest on still, though freezin',
   Thinkin' only of little Bell,
Till breathless, and almost lifeless,
   At 'Bijah's feet he fell,
A-pantin' the fearful message
   He had scarce the breath to tell,
While the little hands, white an' rattlin',
   Told 'Bijah what befell.

"Quickly in snow he held them then,
   And chafed the stiffenin' form,
Wrappin' around the slender child
   His thick frock, nice and warm.
Then, close in his strong arms claspin' him,
   Hurried so swiftly home,
Back over a shorter and warmer path
   Than the boy's brave feet had come.

"And all the way he brought him along,
   Never once putting him down,
Suddenly lovin' the fragile child
   On whom he was wont to frown.

The look on that little pallid face
   Was enough to melt a stone,
So happy, so glad, for a little love, —
   Jest what he had never known.

" 'Twas a strange, new light in them blue eyes,
   With tears their lids were wet;
Fearin' to lose the love he'd found,
   . He nestled the closer to get.
While the rough man's tears ever fallin' fast
   On his own and Benny's face,
And he press'd him closer to his heart
   And quickened his swingin' pace.

" Little Bell lived, but Benny, well,
   He better at first have died,
For his little thin hands were taken off,
   And buried side by side.
No one could be kinder than 'Bijah now;
   But he said 'twas all in vain
When he saw them little handless arms
   Movin' about in pain.

" And every blow he had ever struck
   Came back with a fearful smart,
While often that clingin' and wistful look
   Would make him shudder an' start.
One day he could bear it no longer,
   As he sat by the little bed,
So he told his heart and grief to the boy,
   While bitter tears he shed.

" ' If I had hands,' said the little saint,
   ' I'd wipe them tears away;
Stoop lower, and let me kiss them off,
   Don't sob so, 'Bijah, pray!
I was never so happy in all my life
   As on that awful day

When you held me kindly in your arms,
　　A-huggin' me all the way.

" An' now that I'm goin' — I know it well —
　　I don't want you to mourn
'Bout anything you ever said,
　　Or in anger ever done !
Will you bury me close to mother?
　　Come closer — I — can't — see — plain ; ·
And — hug — me — once — before — I go —
　　I — shall not — mind — the pain ! '

" And he lifted his little handless arms
　　Both by 'Bijah's face,
While strong arms held him gently
　　For his last and faint embrace.
He kissed that rough face soothingly,
　　And then the white arms fell,
And so pleadin' as there they told it,
　　His story I cannot tell."

———ooɔɔǫɔoo———

A MEMORY.

1865—APRIL 14—1878.

It is night on the Appomattox, —
　　A happy and joyful night ;
Faces are glad, yet thoughtful,
　　Around the camp-fire light ;
For Lee has surrendered his legions,
　　The day of strife is past ;
And on the retiring tempest
　　The bow of peace bends at last.

But what is this ominous message
   Trembling over the wires?
What fearful thing sets flashing
   Those mystic signal fires?
And why those muttered curses
   From lips that are not profane?
Why lips compressed and bleaching,
   And the pallor that speaks of pain?

What is whispered from one to another
   In an agony of fear?
" The President *assassinated!* "
   Are the fearful words we hear.
Grim fires gleam in the gloaming,
   The pines sigh overhead,
And our hearts are filled with horror —
   Numb with nameless dread.

The sun that shines on the morrow
   Lights many a saddened camp,
And hearts heavy in unison
   With the sentry's measured tramp.
In suspense we await the message
   The day will surely bring;
The nightmare of fear hangs over
   The day as a fateful thing.

The mute wires tell the message;
   The signal flag dips o'erhead;
The head-quarters flag is lowered, —
   So we know that *Lincoln is dead!*
Pent curses are whispered and muttered
   With a nervous clenching of hands;
With musket at trail and motionless,
   Unrebuked the sentry stands.

God pity the wretch! if that moment
   He had chanced in our hands to fall,

He had gone unshriven to judgment,
  Without coffin, or prayer, or pall.
The star of peace that shone brightly
  Is covered with mist and dim,
The bow from the cloud has vanished
  Because of our tears for him.

O Martyr Emancipator!
  Our hands bring laurels now;
The years but brighten the lustre
  Of thine immortal brow.
Oh, hail him and crown him, comrades!
  His sad face smiles on us still,
And lights up the ominous darkness
  Of days that presage ill.

And we swear, in the light of his teaching,
  No blunder, or worse, shall wrest
From the land or the race he ennobled
  His priceless and deathless bequest.
His foes may exult and triumph,
  Plan plunder or treason still,
They must learn, in Union and *Liberty*
  Alone abide peace and good-will.

IN MEMORIAM.

Rear the white marble shaft solemnly over them;
Scatter sweet spring blossoms tenderly over them;
Thunder of cannon no more shall awaken them, —
In glory and fame the grave hath taken them.

Your tears and your sighs even cannot revive them,
Nor sneers of foes of glory deprive them; —
As firm as this granite their loyal devotion,
As pure as this marble their hearts' warm devotion.

Tear off the crape from your bright silken banners!
Rend the blue air with your deafening hosannas!
Bid the loud bugle with no dead march unman us,
But blare in accord with these star-spangled banners.

Their sons, not their sires, to-day weep above them;
Grief-stricken wives more devotedly love them,
As we with deep reverence stand uncovered above them,
For the years as they fly more gloriously prove them.

Then dash the swift tear that courses unbidden,
And smile over sorrow and griefs canker-hidden; —
And swear here, the sons standing proudly above them,
That no threat of Treason ever shall move them.

Then tune your glad strains to the thunder of cannon,
To Treason's vile head lay the patriot's ban on;
And tear with our Eagle's red beak and black talon
The heart from the traitor, or brand him a felon!

[Written for the dedication of the Soldiers' Monument, Dover, N.H., 1877, but
"The Soldiers' Monument" written and read instead.]

------ ००ஃ०० ------

CANNON, '62–'79.

READ AT THE WEIR'S REUNION, '79.

'62.

To the thunder of cannon we gathered
   Mid the screaming of shot and shell,
And around us youthful heroes
   Like the leaves of autumn fell;
Our skies by the tempest were darkened,
   Portentous of fearful doom,
   nd they cast over youthful fancies
   The pall of a horrible gloom.

For the Flag and the Nation were menaced,
   To be severed, aye, rent in twain!
The dream of our forefathers threatened,
   Should Yorktown's blood be in vain?
Had Washington wasted the counsel
   Which his compatriots heard?
Should the sons of sires who were heroes
   Be no more to loyalty stirred?

And four red years gave answer
   With one-fourth of a million dead;
And to-day who loves his country
   May proudly lift his head
In any of all the nations
   That crowd the populous earth,
Nor blush for our starry emblem,
   Nor blush for the land of our birth.

'79.

And now, to the thunder of cannon
   We gather by Northern lake,
To kindle in peace our camp-fires,
   And the rolling echoes to wake
Over glen and glade and mountain,
   And along the peaceful shore,
As erst we heard them with meaning
   In the battle's deadly roar.

Each gun that thunders a welcome
   To our hero-guests to-day,
To them and to all who hear it
   Let its red tongue leap to say,
"A nation! a nation! a nation!
   Assail, and I speak to slay,
And send shot instead of welcome
   On deadly and direful way."

Speak out then, iron prophet!
In short, sententious speech
To the veterans here assembled;
Bring reminders to all and to each
Of the days when you spake against treason
In such savage and deadly tongue
That all who heard your message
Henceforth its meaning have known.

———oo¦o¦oo———

ENGLAND IN THE ORIENT.

It reads like a tale of enchantment,
Or old Arabian Nights;
Like a scene that flashes and dazzles
In the conqueror's scenic lights;
But Fate stands clear and undoubted,
The power which rules the seas
Unfurls her banner in triumph
In the Oriental breeze.

A Crusade, allied to commerce,
Shall seize the Holy Land,
And wrest the holy sepulchre
From the Moslem's bloody hand.
And along the banks of Euphrates
Shall civilization bloom,
And dispel from early Eden
The Crescent's night of gloom.

Again on the heights of Salem
The temple of God may rise,
And gleam, as of old, in splendor,
Under Judean skies.

And a God-fearing, worshipping people
  Unto Zion may return,
And again on the ancient altar
  The incense of worship burn.

What meaneth England's triumph?
  And what her godly queen?
Why through long fateful centuries
  Still flashes her falchion's sheen?
Was it that, when the moment
  Of a land's deliverance came,
She then might stand to rekindle
  The old historic flame?

A Christian queen! the protectoress
  Of Christian subjects there,
Is more than entered their hearts' desire
  In faith's most earnest prayer.
And eyes that have wept in sorrow,
  Hearts that were heavy with fears,
Are smiling to-day in gladness
  Through joy-begotten tears.

Why, Disraeli, of Israel,
  Like Joseph, or Mordecai, stands
Highest and first in council
  In a far and foreign land,
But there to unfold the purposes,
  Unseen of human eyes,
Which God still keeps before him
  While nations fall and rise.

And what the advance of nations
  Throughout the populous world;
Our own great war for freedom,
  Our banner in peace unfurled?
What mean the triumphs of science?
  That we to-day may stand

And read the fate which yesterday
  Brought to the Holy Land.

India, now in the fingers
  Of England's royal hand,
And Cyprus the thumb that encloses
  And clasps the historic land.
Her argosies ride in triumph
  Where the Pharaoh's legions trod,
Where the Red Sea's waves closed over
  The hosts which fought against God.

A world-wide dominion and kingdom!
  The old Israelitist dream,
In which Jehovah is worshipped
  As God, over all — supreme!
Does it wait on the verge of fulfilment?
  Has the pride of the Gentiles come
To stand in reverent worship
  And rear again the dome

Which Roman legions levelled?
  It is well to pause, and turn
The leaves of the scroll of the prophets
  Who spake that man may learn,
For if God *is God*, and ruler
  Of the old historic land,
Nor flag, nor sword, shall raise therefor
  Without his guiding hand.

NO DANGER.

"Hush, Grace! the baby'll be better;
   The doctor told me so.
I'll not be out late, surely;
   I promised, or would not go."
His form was erect and manly,
   His glance was steady and clear,
Yet the young wife's heart was heavy
   With a shrinking nameless fear.

Only a little feverish;
   "No danger" — the doctor said;
But ere the midnight hour had come
   He stood again by the bed,
Where the little one tossed in anguish,
   Crying out for breath and air;
And while the mother was frantic,
   The father was not there.

He sits among boon companions,
   Flushed with gaming and drink,
Of wife and dying baby
   He pauses not to think.
A brawl, — the lie, — and a pistol shot
   Cuts into his clustering curls,
And sense and sensation forsake him, —
   The scene into darkness whirls.

The last resort in the baby's case —
   The little white throat is bare,
The silver tube is inserted
   To give the sufferer air.
His reason clear, his brown eyes bright,
   His lips move to say "papa" —
He longs for his father's kiss,
   And pleads with his eyes for papa.

Heavy steps cease at the doorway,
 ·The door-bell loudly rings, —
The time is the gray of morning,
 Which this horrible burden brings,
The little eyes still pleading for father,
 He wistfully looks again,
His brave heart longs to hear his step .
 But listens and waits in vain.

Father is there but his eyes are closed
 In a stunned and sottish sleep,
And mother alone with breaking heart
 Her vigil of love must keep.
With love for a thousand and kisses for two,
 She hangs o'er the sufferer's bed,
As speechless lips and pleading eyes
 Drift away to the dream of the dead.

He puts up his speechless lips for a kiss,
 Soothes his mother with tender hand,
Caressing her face and neck like this, —
 His eyes fix on vacancy — and
The wounded father's boy is dead.
 The father, unconscious, breathes heavy and slow,
The mother a maniac wild —
 While neither their dead boy know.

The morn brings the father's reason,
 The night was a horrible dream,
 wife's good-by — a baby's moan —
 A flash and a blade's bright gleam.
He wakes with a bandaged head,
 A shattered and bleeding hand,
While watchful and sad attendants
 Expectant around him stand.

He calls for Grace and the baby —
 They put his inquiries by

Until the day of the burial
  When he stands tottering nigh,
While prayer and funeral rites consign
  His boy to an early grave,
And him to a life of anguish
  From which no hand can save.

We wonder not that in after years
  He hates and shuns the bowl,
Which casts such withering, cursing blight
  Upon body and home and soul.
When fair lips say, " No danger,"
  Wine flashing in jewelled hands,
Is it strange that a pallor comes o'er his face,
  That he like statue stands?

From fire like this sad scene
  Are Temperance apostles born,
Whose homes and hopes are blasted,
  Whose hearts are bleeding and torn.
May that devil's lie of " No danger "
  Rob no more homes of bliss,
Lead no more hearts to the gilded dens
  Where wine serpents crawl and hiss.

TO THE MOWERS.

At morn we hear the mower's song
  We hear the scythe's sharp ring,
And thoughts go out to absent boys,
  Who other weapons swing ;
Who grasped with us these weapons here
  But two short years ago ;
And think the change of harvests strange
  Which you are called to now.

When in the sultry summer's air
   We hear the insects hum,
Our toil with yours we oft compare,
   The bees' drone with the drum!
And if we tire in toils of peace,
   Or faint in Northern fields,
We scorn the wish which seeks relief
   While you such weapons wield.

The grain is ripening in the field,
   The harvest groweth brown;
A symbol of the rebel host,
   And of their going down.
We think of belching batteries' roar
   On hill and mountain side,
Of swaths made by the screeching shell,
   Red with the battle's tide.

We think of the sabre's deadly thrust,
   The rifle's rattling noise,
And, as we wipe the tears away,
   Ask, "Where are now the boys?"
When from the stench of battle-field
   You fain would turn away,
Comes e'er a fragrant memory
   Of clover-scented hay?

Oh, nerve your hearts like beaten steel
   To meet each coming blow,
And you shall see Rebellion reel; —
   At word we wait to go!
Remember we have heard the call,
   That soon we'll be with you,
And grasp the soldier's harvest scythe
   To mow the rebel crew.

AUG., 1863.

THE MIDNIGHT BUGLE.

(A DREAM.)

I heard the voice of a bugle
  That sounded through the land,
From Washington to Oregon,
  From Maine to the Rio Grande;
And the lips that blew that summons
  Were bloodless, thin, and white,
And the spectre vanished in darkness
  Of the weird and lone midnight.

To the nation's living sleepers
  The sound was all unheard,
But the earth over every soldier dead
  At that strange summons stirred;
And forth from those thousand nameless mounds
  By the broad Potomac's side,
And forth from those wide and gastly pits
  By the Rappahannock's tide.

And from under marble monuments
  From over all the North,
The hosts of slain to life again
  From bivouac came forth;
And they marched in the midnight silence,
  Nor uttered e'er a word;
And the horses slain with their riders
  Were seen, but were not heard.

Their tattered battle banners
  From the nation's halls they took,
And forth in silence beneath the stars
  Their blackened folds they shook.
Hatless and shoeless, with pale white feet,
  Over the grasses of June,

They marched with measured cadence
    To the soul of martial tune.

Unused and rusty armor
    In haste they buckle on,
Sheathed sword, and shouldered musket,
    And straight away were gone.
The guns of blackened batteries
    And caissons in line were wheeled,
And murdered gunners mounted them,
    And rode as for the field.

And up from the Hampton waters
    The sunken Cumberland came,
And there trod the deck in silence,
    Who sank with her the same ;
Straight for Mount Vernon, silently,
    Swiftly away she sailed,
Under the guns of grim Monroe,
    Nor answered she nor hailed.

" Summon them from their slumber,
    The hosts by treason slain ;
Summon and bring them ! *Every man*
    Is needed for duty again ! "
From the tomb upon Mount Vernon,
    From a voice we need not name,
The order went forth to the Nation's dead,
    And thither in ranks they came.

Where the first or last dead commanders
    Were riding side by side,
And there passed before them, in review,
    Our heroes, true and tried ;
There was whispered to each, " The Union ! "
    From the nation's sacred grave ;
While "Law forever and Liberty ! "
    For countersign they gave.

"For the front!" and away towards Washington
  Battalions wheel again,
And they march inspired as the soul of one —
  One fourth of a million men.
"Go! put the sword to treason, —
  A sword that is swift to slay ;
Sweep the capital clean of corruption
  Before the light of day.

" Post guards at doors of the White House,
  And guards at the Senate Hall,
And guards in the other chamber,
  And be they true men, all !
To every hamlet in the land
  A silent sentinel send,
On every hill, in every vale,
  To walk till time shall end !"

And ever more at midnight hour,
  Defiles this sad " relief;"
And then the relieved return to salute
  The first and the Martyr Chief.
Lo ! mothers and fathers by those posts
  Shall wait for fallen sons,
And children watch in silent awe
  For the gleam of their spectre guns.

JUNE, 1878.

FIGHT YOUR WAY UP.

Inch by inch you must win your way,
　　By steady and sturdy blows;
Scornful alike of fawning friends
　　Or the sneer of incredulous foes.
You may not pause to be lifted,
　　Nor the nectar of dalliance sup,
But, with firm and relentless endeavor,
　　Fight your way steadily up.

Indolence, envy, and malice,
　　The open or covert attack,
Will meet you at every footfall, —
　　Even friends will hold you back.
But grim, relentless, and earnest,
　　From the shadow into the light,
If you rise at all you rise because
　　Of dauntless and upward fight.

The laurel bay and crown await,
　　But rugged paths and steep
Will mock all puny effort,
　　While fate her guard doth keep.
Then nerve your hand with iron will,
　　Strong to caress or smite,
For you alone reach crown and bay
　　By steady and stalwart fight.

BIRCH ISLAND TROUT.

A prince among fish is the trim lake trout,
   He strikes with a vigorous vim;
And you must know well what you're about
   To succeed in hooking him.

But give me the other trout,
   The trout of the mountain brook,
That gleams through the black pool in and out,
   With a dash at your bated hook.

Then here's to the trout, be he little or big,
   In lake or in mountain brook,
If he dance in a net to the fisherman's jig,
   Or go it alone on a hook!

So yellow and luscious, so dainty and rare,
   So crisp if he's done to a turn;
Perhaps nature furnishes sport more rare,
   But that we have yet to learn.

There may be a daintier, choicer dish,
   For the palate of the epicure;
But if so, we have never heard of the fish,
   Nor shall we ever, I am sure.

J. WILSON BARRON.

Brave Barron! with blue eye undaunted,
   When the rope tightened round your neck,
Was there naught in its martyr pleading
   The murderer's purpose to check?
From the vault where you faithfully guarded
   The trusts of your humble bank
A spirit went forth well worthy
   With heroes and martyrs to rank.

And they must make room in heaven
   For a hero in honor high,
One more with the chivalric courage,
   At the post of duty to die.
We will blush less now for the faithless,
   Defaults and embezzlements rife,
And point with pride to the hero
   Who defended his trust with his life.

And we will thank God for Christian honor,
   And courage, that men though dead
Take new faith in human nature
   From your bruised and wounded head;
And will answer the sneer of the cynic,
   Who says, "Every man has his price;
Religion! a sham and delusion! —
   A defaulter's deceitful device?"

Remember the brave man, Barron,
   With sense of honor so high,
That guarding the trusted treasure,
   He was ready and strong to die.
Make room for a civic hero,
   In America's temple of fame,
An untitled New England baron,
   Well worthy the title to claim.

Make room for a Christian hero !
   Away with the libellous lie
That *all* are too callous for honor,
   Too sordid for duty to die.
Friend Murray, this man was a deacon,
   Let the world give the Church its due,
And weep with us who knew him,
   For a heart strong as steel and as true.

DON'T WAIT TILL THEY'RE DEAD.

If you have a neighbor near you
   Trying to lift up his head,
And a kind word or look will help him,
   Pray, don't wait till he is dead
Before you recognize him,
   And speak your word of cheer,
But do it now, frank and cheerful, —
   Do it while he is *here*.

The world has been full of this waiting, —
   To the shame of men be it said ! —
Before they do a man justice
   They wait, as a rule, till he's dead.
Withholding all helpful sympathy,
   Sometimes even bread ;
And then they will build a monument,
   After the toiler is dead.

How many brave hearts have struggled,
   With brave and hopeful tread,
Waiting man's tardy justice,
   Winning life's scanty bread,

As well worthy of bay and laurels,
  Struggling, toiling ahead,
As when a marble monument
  Rises to tell — *they are dead.*

Look around you, then, and never
  Give reason to have it said
That you waited without recognition
  Until your neighbor was dead.
Go and give now your greeting,
  With generous words, instead
Of waiting, as most have waited,
  Until the toiler was dead.

It may be a wife or daughter,
  Passing, with patient tread,
The round of life's simple duties,
  With hearts as heavy as lead ;
With hands that never falter,
  With aching and weary head,
While waiting your recognition,
  Receiving but coldness instead.

It may be a husband or father,
  Or brother, whom you have led,
Who waits with wistful pleading
  For the word you have not said.
Oh, wait no longer ! life passes, —
  Its hours will soon have sped, —
Delay not your heart's kind prompting ;
  Don't wait till they are dead.

It is strange how soon and surely,
  After death has claimed his own,
The world remembers their virtues,
  And speaks what it has known.
It seems I have seen a smile lurking,
  Lighting up a dead cold face

In scorn of the tardy mockery
　　They knew to be taking place.

Go with niggardly words no longer
　　For those who toil by your side,
Waiting, without commendation,
　　Till the tired toilers have died;
Meet them and greet them frankly,
　　Encourage while they are here,
And see the face sad and thoughtful,
　　Break into a smile of cheer.

Wait not till hope has vanished,
　　Till hearts, from neglect, have bled;
Wait not till earth is dreary,
　　Till gloom gathers overhead;
Wait not till feet worn and weary,
　　By the hand of Fate are led,
Sad and mutely, despairing
　· Down into the rest of the dead;

Before you give generous greeting, —
　　Chasing the ghoul of fear, —
Before you witness the grateful
　　Smile of faces really dear;
But with eyes beaming glad recognition,
　　Faithful, and frank, and clear,
Dispense to each toiler around you
　　Your helpful and hopeful cheer.

　　　　　　——∞◦◦◦∞——

REST.

O hills of my boyhood, I greet you again!
　· Let me rest on your broad, brown sides!
Oh take from my heart this wearying pain
　　While the sun o'er your round crest rides!

Of brown Earth's bosom the cheering fount,
   On you my head I rest;
Though weary footsteps tardily mount
   To the joy of your nourishing breast.

Fold ye, and hold me in sheltering arms;
   To your grand maternity press;
Till you soothe from my heart all sad alarms
   With the peace of your blesséd caress.

To the sting of disease thy healing balm
   In the fulness of faith I bind;
Nor doubt I in thy restful calm
   The joy of healing to find.

STARS FOR THE CROWN.

A CHRISTMAS LESSON.

PRELUDE.

Long hate the Prophets ceased to warn,
   And Faith in doubt was shrouded;
To those who waited for the morn
   The heavens were darkly clouded.
The valley held the Lily's bloom,
   Waiting, wan, and wearied,
Lebanon's cedars stood in gloom,
   While the Redeemer tarried.
The glory of Zion seemed afar,
   The night held not its gem,
And, while it waited the Morning Star,
   Knew not its Bethlehem.

The mantle of night lay on the plain,
    The stars above shone clear,
In sparkling welcome of the strain,
    Ere they of earth could hear.
For lo! the lost song of their morning joy
    Again in the heavens is ringing;
Well may the vaulted heavens employ
    The whole of their hosts in singing
The glad anthem of joy again —
    "Peace on earth; good will toward men."

Shout the glad message, ye sons of God!
    Sing ye stars with them!
Mercy now stays the chastening rod,
    Christ is born in Bethlehem!
"Glory to God!" sang the angel choirs;
    "Glory to God!" sang the answering stars;
"Glory to God!" flashed the beacon fires
    To heavens remotest bars.
Rang the grand choral of joy again,
    "Peace on earth; good will toward men."

It seemed sadly in vain;
For the innocent slain
Mothers in sorrow are weeping;
    Sharon's opening bud
    To be crushed in blood, —
With sin, was in sorrowful keeping.
So, fitly for aye, at Christmas time,
May we gladden the heart of the Child,
For the first martyrs now, near the throne sublime,
From the hand of a Herod, red with crime,
    Came up from that massacre wild.
And He who escaped till the day of his death
Spake with his own dear, life-giving breath
    The sweetest words He has given,
"Suffer the children to come unto me,
    They must not be forbidden;

So the hearts of all who come must be,
    Of such is the kingdom of heaven."

    But His own face yet,
    With His own blood wet,
Must be laid in bitterest anguish down ;
There is buffet and insult, scourging and scorn,
The mock robe of royalty, crown of thorn,
Ere he wears by right the Redeemer's crown.

He groans in agony, wild and aloud,
The thorn-torn head in death is bowed.
The dumb earth answers its Maker's moan,
A low dirge the stars of the morning moan,
And shed in shame their pitying tears,
While God's mercy mantles this crime of the years.
And they bore Him away to the waiting tomb ;
The Rose and the Lily came not to bloom.

But the work of the Master is not complete ;
They must hear the tread of those buried feet ;
They must see the light of those closed eyes ;
From the gloom of that death He must arise.
They must hear again the matchless voice,
Ere in Christ, as "God with us," they fully rejoice.
From Edom, and Bozrah, in garments red,
    They hear from the door of the opening grave,
The sound of His footsteps, welcoming tread,
    Who speaks now in righteousness, mighty to save.

" Reach hither thy hand to this pierced palm,
    Thrust it into the wound of the Roman spear,
That the surge of your sad doubts I may calm,
    And take from your hearts your blinding fear.
And lo ! I am with you unto the end ;
    Go with the glad tidings afar,
For healing and life the Word shall attend,
And ye shall know well what meaneth, ' The Friend
    That is closer than brothers are.' "

The angels are waiting with honor to greet,
    Yet hushed is their triumphant psalm,
While gratitude covers with tears the feet,
    Wounded in bringing to earth a balm.
Wide are now swinging the portal doors,
    And the golden gates are lifted high;
There are palms and crowns on the golden floors,
    For the Victor Prince is nigh.
Lift higher your heads, ye glorious gates,
Before you, to enter, the Conqueror waits;
Higher and higher till He enters in,
From the fearful contest with death and sin.

Centurial ages have passed away
Since they steadfastly gazed into heaven that day,
But the Master hath promised, and still He guides;
And here on this gladsome Christmas eve
Into every heart that will believe
He silently enters and there abides.

THE LESSON.

Still soundeth that mystic minstrelsy,
    —"Forever, to-day, and yesterday,"—
And Conscience, the wakeful shepherd, keeps
Unwearied vigil while Reason sleeps,
And ever in times of the spirit's calm,
With the power and spell of a soothing charm,
If the soul will listen, it still is there,
The soundless song, on the midnight air.
And though those angels grand and olden,
Who flashed from portals gemmed and golden,
Have never repeated to mortal ear
The song of that night, so sweet and clear, —
Though never again to mortal eyes
Have given one gleam of their angel guise, —
Still, on the air o'er the slum'brous soul,
Broken strains of that symphony, silently roll;

Who hears their song on this sorrowing earth,
May know that it heralds a Saviour's birth.
Well may this heraldry banish fears,
For the cradle of Christ is the heart that hears.

To one listening life this music came
    With all its meaning manifold,
Imparting the glow of a heavenly flame,
    And more of joy than heart could hold,
The golden bowl brimming to overflow.
Surely, sorrow need only know
There was light for night,
And life for death,
And a song of joy,
For sorrow's breath;
A soul redeemed, its sins forgiven,
A glimpse of the many-mansioned heaven,
To gladly receive the tidings given.
It seemed to His early love that all
Must yield their hearts to the gentle call:
"They perish now, Master, in pain and woe;"
And his prayer was pleading "Oh, bid me go!"

The Lord Christ heard, as the rapt youth prayed,
A sweet smile over His features played;
On the low bowed head of his weeping child,
His piercéd hand tenderly left a blessing;
    While the answering voice so clear and mild,
    Thrilled, with joy that was almost wild,
The heart that was dumb with delight, while pressing
His head now raised to that blessèd rest,
Which is known when pillowed upon His breast
And he heard the warning:
                "Would you know
That the world has sin as well as woe;
That many will scorn both the message and thee;
That the rage of their madness died not with me:
That still there is possible Calvary?"

" Thou shalt go, my son, but with me awhile,
You must learn the spell of the tempter's wile,
Which is over the world and even thee : —
I will teach you how they welcome me."
And clasped in the strength of encircling arms,
    He felt on his brow the Saviour's kiss,
That sealed him safe from the tempter's charms,
    • With a foretaste faint of heaven's bliss.

They went where the great world's thoughtless throngs
Sped on to the grave with laughter and songs.
There the Lord himself called, and called in vain.
The enthusiast heart was torn with pain,
As he said, "O Master! why must they die?
Let us stand in their path, and strive, and cry."
But swifter and swifter it sped along ;
For answer, some strain of a bacchanal song.
Their effort was futile, they could not detain
The throngs of that passional pleasure train.
Faint and far in the distance their voices were lost,
And life was the price which this madness cost.
There were rulers and statesmen hurrying past ;
Not a look on the patient pleader cast.

From this thoughtless revel the young man turned ;
With deep indignation his spirit burned ;
    He had heard them there with foul scoffing deride,
    And curse with the name of the Crucified ;
    While scorn with hate exultingly vied,
Love deeper than his was lightly spurned.
" Why, some would crucify now, I fear,
For the warning you speak so kindly here."
But he meets, as he listens with strange surprise,
A keen rebuke in the low replies.

" My child, though scorned, I come each day,
And call to the throngs that crowd this way.

For anon, when these fair cheeks are paling,
And the joy of this false lure is failing,
Some will call with hopeless wailing.
Whenever they call, I wait to go —
And am only sad when they scorn me so."
The zeal of impatience in shame is weeping;
While the vigil of pity the Christ is keeping.

" Let us turn to those who have wisely heard,
And heeded the call of the living Word.
Your spirit would falter and faint, I fear,
If I were to teach you only here.
My children have reared a temple of praise,
Where they gather to worship on holy days."

Gay doors are closed, the marts are still,
The bells of the Sabbath quietly thrill
The air, and hearts, and hurrying feet,
That river of life in the silent street.
They have gathered from many a home of prayer;
The strong and the aged, the young and the fair,
In reverent silence are waiting there.
The great organ breathes out its suppliant strain,
   A sound like the pleading of many souls,
   As through the high arches its melody rolls,
Then sobs its low prayer into silence again.

By prayer the worshipping throng is led,
The Word, with reverent heeding read ;
Then an anthem of praise whose choral swell,
Voices the worshipping host so well.
Now, from lips where the Master's touch has stayed,
   From heart that His deathless love has fired,
From mind which saving truth has swayed,
   From soul, by the strength of faith inspired,
Came the spoken Word with power endued,
By the blood of the Crucified deeply imbued.

Even while He plead there were answering sighs,
And tears were falling from soulful eyes.
They were fired with the joy the Saviour sends,
When the worshipper low in penitence bends.

The heart of the young disciple was filled
With an ecstatic longing and fervor thrilled,
As anew for the work of his life he burned;
And, again to Him who had led him there he turned,
While his heart and features were all aglow,
For this must gladden the sad one so.
But the touching sadness remained the same,
Though he greeted with joy Love's bursting flame.

"My child, I am glad for these and thee,
But through this worshipping throng I see
The sad homes of the children of poverty.
They have barred by these grand and massive doors
The steps that would stain these muffled floors, —
The paths which my earthly footsteps trod
Lead not to this, though the house of God.
And while I am glad for this scene to-day, —
Glad when the rich and gifted pray,
My heart for the poor and the humble bleeds, —
The gulf is wide from this to their needs."

The listener clasped his hands in prayer;
         Into his heart as never before
         Came the Spirit that seeks the humble door.
"Bid me to the lowly thy message bear;
I will walk till my feet be bare and bleeding,
If thou wilt grant thy blessed leading!"
Then over that face a new light stole,
That flooded with peace that pleading soul;
He rests, as John, in a moment of bliss,
And his lips were scaled by a sacred kiss.

"Thus do I," He said, slow and solemnly,
"Consecrate thee to this blessed ministry;

Thy lips thus sealed shall never plead
In vain with the chldren of toil and need;
I have given this consecration holy,
Let the words of thy mouth be pure and lowly; —
Even now I will lead you to win the first gem
With which I will fill your diadem."
Past stately abodes of plenty, of pride,
    Where were ringing the sounds of Christmas cheer, —
    For the morrow would bring that a day so dear, —
Wondering he followed the steps of his guide,
To a place that wronged the name of home;
To the depths for priceless pearls they come.

A worn mother watches a fluttering breath,
O'er her pale infant struggling with death.
The breath of the drinker has left its blight,
And banished the lustre of Love's quiet light.
A face, full of longing, so shrunken and pale,
As no words can tell, told the sorrowful tale;
There was no food nor warmth for the dying child
Whose piteous wail was driving her wild.
Unconscious the while in a sottish sleep
Lay the woman's protector, — "To cherish and keep."
How vain that sacred nuptial vow
Seemed to that wronged woman now.
The only comfort in this her grief,
This drunken slumber was real relief.
In vain the aid so kindly brought —
The light, the warmth and nursing — were naught
To stay the destroyer.   The child was dead!
In mercy, soon from its misery sped.
One thought of the day of betrothal to him
Now unconscious, and all grew dim; —

For pale and still as her dead child there,
The mother fell back in a swoon of despair;
But the spell on the stupid sleeper is past,
From a base debauch, awake at last,

To behold the wreck his life had wrought,
To be by this fearful ruin taught.
For a moment he sat in silence there, —
He had known her when young and saintly fair,
And had loved her long and loved her well,
Till held in the chains of that demon spell, —
Back to those bright and happy years,
His conscience scourged; with remorseful tears
He plead for one look, one answering word,
Till the thoughtful strangers turned away,
Thinking God and conscience wiser than they.
Her closed eyes opened, unrebuking and mild,
They lingered a moment on father and child,
Then closed amid such a pallor of woe,
As only the patient, heart-broken know.

"My God! I thank thee," said the now earnest man,
And he spake as only the fervid can;
"And here by the side of my dead, I swear
To follow no more this path of despair."
But the "Man of Sorrows," who has watched the fears
Of eighteen hundred circling years
To enter this life, is waiting here;
        His locks were white with the cares he bore,
        The dews of night had sprinkled them o'er;
        His kind hand knocked at the closed door
Of the strong man's heart — unknown, and so near.
With earnest pleading, and tender tone,
While sorrow is reaping what sin has sown,
He says to the heart with agony full,
"Though as scarlet now, it shall be as wool.
Long, so long ere this sorrowful day
I sought, and in scorn you turned away;
But now, my sadly erring son,
Despite the wrong you have madly done,
I love, and would save you from your sin;
Let me into your heart. Oh, let me in!"

One long, fierce struggle with self and pride, —
    The spell is broken, — the will is bowed,
And the tender arms of the Crucified
    Clasp that strong penitent, weeping aloud.

The mother's eyes brimmed with a holy joy;
    Her torn heart throbbed with a blissful pain
    As she lifted her thought in thanks again,
For that angel of mercy, — her dear dead boy.

The hours had sped, and midnight morn,
    From the hours of Christmas eve had come;
And lo! again was Jesus born,
    In one more heart in a humble home.

From the blessèd glow of that heavenly light
The disciple went forth to a storm-torn night;
Swiftly aslant through the silent street
The cold wind blew the stinging sleet;
But he heeded it not, for there by his side
Was the silent step of the Crucified.
And the calm delight in the Master's eyes
Filled his soul with glad surprise.

"Thy sorrow, thy joy, thou knowest now;
With this first star I crown thy brow."

ON AN INVITATION TO WRITE.

The fire that burns and brightens
  May not be kindled at will,
It burneth hot, unasked, unsought,
  When the tongue is mute and still.
From sights and sounds we stumble on,
  From thorns that tear the heart; —
We smite when the iron is white with heat; —
  This is the poet's art.
    It can't be run off by the yard, man,
      We don't run it off by the yard;
    He who can has no claim of poet,
      He is only a calico bard.

He who says we feel not our fancies, —
  That fancy which paints the page, —
Is cool, and stirs not, nor trembles
  With things of which we rage;
Knows not of the thorns that tear us,
  Naught of our hours of pain,
Nor of the laughter which shakes us
  When satire's page we stain.
    It can't be run off by the yard, man,
      We don't run it off by the yard;
    He who can has no claim of poet,
      He is only a calico bard.

When fire unseen is kindled
  Our own hearts throb and bleed;
Or satire grim point to the hymn
  We sing from our own heart's need.
We sing on, though no one listens,
  We sing though no one cares;
Glad when the reader's eye glistens,
  Or a smile some sad face wears.

It can't be run off by the yard, man,
　We don't run it off by the yard;
He who can has no claim of poet,
　He is only a calico bard.

So, ask of me not a measure,
　Set me no stilted task;
You know not the way of our fancies,
　You know not what you ask.
True songs are not made to order,
　They're born, they are not made;
They run not in grooves of traffic; —
　Poetry isn't a trade.
　　It can't be run off by the yard, man,
　　　We don't run it off by the yard;
　　He who can has no claim of poet,
　　　He is only a calico bard.

The poet must be a creator,
　Or paint such scenes as he sees;
Or pierce with rhythmic satire, —
　He writes not alone to please.
But when, with tears or laughter,
　You greet what we send to you,
You know we drink of waters
　Whose source you may not view.
　　It can't be run off by the yard, man,
　　　We don't run it off by the yard;
　　He who can has no claim of poet,
　　　He is only a calico bard.

MEMORIAL HYMN.

We wait now with weeping,
Where heroes brave are sleeping,
Who live in song and story,
And deeds of fadeless glory.
　　Though dead they live, to memory dear,
　　The nation's dead are resting here.

A wreath for brows immortal,
We twine around death's portal,
And leave it here above them,
To show that still we love them;
　　Though dead they live, to memory dear,
　　The nation's dead are resting here.

The past comes up before us, —
Our battle flag is o'er us;
The battle call is sounding,
And men to death are bounding;
　　Though dead they live, to memory dear,
　　The nation's dead are resting here.

In peace sublime above us,
Unseen they wait and love us;
And there we hope to meet them;
In heaven's peace to greet them;
　　Though dead they live, to memory dear,
　　The nation's dead are resting here.

THE BURNING VILLAGE.

[Written on the Farmington fire, Feb., 1875.   Printed for citizens, and read at
dedication of new Congregational Church.]

Startled from sleep, you woke to dream
What seems to you yet a frightful dream ;
The clang of the bell
Came down through the night,
In terror to tell
Its tale of affright,
By the startling glare and gleam
Of billows of leaping light.

And there alone the sentinel spire
Flashed forth to view from a sea of fire ;
And the tone of the bell,
Like a human tone,
Had its tale to tell,
With a shriek and groan,
Like an impotent fierce desire
Pulsed forth from a heart of stone.

The startled multitude stood appalled,
With hands and hearts in fear enthralled ;
And the gilded vane,
In wild alarm,
Trembled with pain,
From fear of harm,
While the bell still clamored and called   .
For help from a powerless arm.

Higher and higher the tongues of fire
Leapt up and crept up roof and spire,
Till the stars of heaven,
And the red fire stars,

Seemed mingled and driven; .
And fiery bars
Were hurled by the wind's fierce ire,
Till they floated, far up, like stars.

In an hour the blistering breath passed by,
And under a midnight arctic sky,
In place of your temple
Was left alone
But ashes trampled
And crumbling stone,
And tears you might well be blinded by,
. And the homeless worshippers' moan.

A year has fled since that night of fear,
And temple and turret are builded here;
Temple and tower
And roof and wall;
A bell tells the hour
From turret tall;
It stands complete the toil of a year,
To sound forth the Master's call.

And now, as you gather here to-day,
To hallow the altar where men shall pray,
Bring only your pure gold,
Purged as by fire;
Let no heart here hold
An unhallowed desire;
Bring self to the altar, and slay;
. Then call for the heavenly fire.

WINGS OF FLAME.

[Delivered at dedication of the Congregational Church, Pittsfield, N.H., Feb. 12, 1877, on the site of one burned one year before in a fearful storm.]

Under the scowl of a winter sky,
A wild snow-tempest roaring by,
  A faint flame creeps,
    With smothered sign,
  While the village sleeps,
    With danger nigh ;
Slowly at midnight the menace creeps
While the village, unconscious of danger, sleeps.

Steady and slow, with flickering glow,
Striking a key-note sure and low,
  The fire-fiend sings
    While beating slow
  His mottled wings,
    That none may know
The terrible tone of the glee he sings,
Nor the fearful sweep of his ghastly wings.

But he breaks his chains and up, away !
No longer imprisoned will tamely stay,
  With open beak
    Upon his prey
  Will fall and shriek
    As up and away
With gleaming talon and bloody beak
To circle and soar with maddening shriek.

And now on the air the dire of bells,
Whose startled tone the danger tells,
  With clang and roar
    The summons swells,
  Pealing out o'er
    The snow-clad dells,

Smiting the red flames' gathering roar,
Sounding loud summons o'er and o'er.

No longer the peaceful village sleeps,
No longer the flame of the burning creeps,
But swift lights flash,
The red light leaps,
While timbers crash
And weakness weeps ;
And into the storm with roar and crash,
Red wings circle and soar and flash.

So, into the night an inverted hell
Kindled its lurid burnings well ;
Red gleams arose
As thick clouds fell
To mingle and close
In the mimic hell,
The gloom of these disclosed by those,
As the steady gleam of the burning rose.

Steadily beating the mad bell rings ;
The tall tower trembles, sways and swings :
Above, the snow
Now melts and clings,
While mad below
The hoarse shout sings ;
Thick in the heavens the clouds of snow,
Reflecting the horror that rolls below.

There are billows of flame, they rush and roar
And crackle and leap till the heavens o'er
Flash grimly back
The horrid glow,
The ruin and rack
That glare below,
The swift storm squadrons dense and black
Reflecting the blood-red gleaming back.

The clinging lips of the furious fire
With passionate, fierce, and fell desire
    Are sated soon ;
      The passion dire
    Is bated soon ;
      A bridal pyre !
And the ravished village is left alone
To sigh and weep with piteous moan.

Temple and mart and dwelling gone,
Blackened cinders on snow-white lawn ;
    And night shuts down
      Till the coming dawn
    Reveals the town
      To the morrow's morn,
The gloom victorious settles down
Over a blackened and ravished town.

But the days of a year fly on their round
With sign of builders on the ground ;
    The structure grows,
      Mid hammers' sound,
    To rival those
      The red flames found,
More stately and grander far than those
Which fell in the burning fearful throes.

Turret and spire and roof and wall,
Chancel and organ, chapel, all
    Await to-day
      The Master's call ;
    We bow and pray
      As low we fall,
Accept Thou what we build to-day ;
Take, and take never Thy grace away.

EARLY POEMS.

REPLY OF NIGHT.

What, O Night! canst thou discover,
   In thy wide extended reign?
What that would delight thee ever; —
   What that thou wouldst not uncover,
Seest thou 'neath thy sweeping train?

I see, the voice of Night replies,
The smiling lands of sunny skies;
The frigid North with icy seas,
Where chill of death floats on the breeze;
I see broad mountains, hill, and vale,
From whence floats up the trusting tale,
That riseth e'er from .the whispering pine,
And the low, sweet tone of the clinging vine;
The musical, murmuring waterfall,
The tremulous notes of the night birds' call;
Scenes and sounds that speak like these,
Breathe of a spirit that can but please.

There is much, however, inquiring bard,
In the beauty of night that man hath marred;
There is much that is sad and wildly strange
Ever within my vision's range, —

Come float with me o'er the busy street,
Where echoes still the tramp of feet; —
There are footfalls firm upon that pave,
And those whose tottering speaks of the grave;

There are eyes that sparkle undimmed by tears,
And hearts that ache with the load of years ;
Virtue unstained in its fountain clear,
And vice in its sickening loathsome leer,
Thoughts like a canker that eat the heart,
From which with a shudder of fear you start ;
Mortal, I would that that hurrying crowd
Just for a moment would think aloud,
That you for a moment might see and know
That unseen current's under-flow ;
Alas ! it is not for mortal ear,
The pulsing, throbbings of thought to hear.

Oh, where are the houses to which this throng,
These lives, these thinking souls belong ?
What joy, and, too, what nameless care,
As guests are with the inmates there !
This scene is but one of those wonders vast
O'er which the folds of my robe are cast ;
They lie unnumbered all over your land, —
On mountain side, by ocean's strand ;
And mingled murmur borne on the breeze
Is floating forever up from these.

There are sounds of wailing that strike the ear ;
The stifled groan, the shriek of fear ;
Sounds that float out o'er the air,
Speaking of sin and deep despair ;
And mingled with these are sounds of mirth,
A medley strange comes up from earth.
List ! there's a low and tremulous voice —
Angels in heaven will now rejoice !
'Tis a young mother's faith that in that tone
Presses her first-born up to the throne.
Another low voice ! it cometh from where
A child is breathing its evening prayer ;
Sweetly solemn, touchingly mild,
Riseth the prayer of the trusting child,

Speaking of childish wants and fears,
With a faith that shameth riper years.
Angels are chanting in heavenly lays,
"Hope for earth, for childhood prays!"

A tableau strange this earth appears,
Mingling mirth, and woe, and prayers.
Mortal, I cannot describe it to you,
The whole a finite may never view!

————oo;o;oo————

MORNING IN SPRING-TIME.

In the east the coming sunlight,
Struggling with the shades receding,
By the pale light's quiet coming,
By the songster's timid warbling,
We may know that shade and darkness
By the morn are being vanquished.
Slowly, though, the night departeth,
Owning that its reign is routed,
Hiding from the coming twilight
To the westward of the mountains,
And amid the thick-boughed forests.
Now the morning brightness stretcheth
Far away unto the westward;
And the shades which slowly left us
Lie along the far horizon,
Fading, sinking, slowly melting,
Blending with the conquering twilight.
All the stars have sought their couches,
Save the few that twinkle faintly
Through the dim dissolving shadows.
In the east the rays shoot upward,
Giving by their sparry splendor,·
To the scene a massive glory.

Where is now the unseen centre
From which such a flood proceedeth?
What great power from out that centre
Forces all that blazing brightness,
So that all the stars attendant
Whirl forever on their courses,
Bathed in this surrounding grandeur,
Smiling back their joyous praises
To that never-failing fountain
Which has clothed their forms with beauty,
Which has life and light imparted?
　While we thus have questioned, musing;
. Lo! the moon has been advancing,
Look along the bright horizon;
That round hill with wood-crowned summit!
Look ye now around the branches,
Where the moon's last shadow perished —
How those strong trees seem to tremble!
How those branchlets seem dissolving!
There the dazzling arching surface
Rising slowly, grandly o'er them,
Leaving all unharmed the forest,
And unmelted the round mountain!
Close your eyes, — you still behold it
With a round screen o'er its surface,
Keeping back the burning brightness,
Save around the glistening edges;
Yes, you see it; still you see it;
With its trembling pendant curtain,
Rising, rising, slowly rising!
　There behold the fiery centre,
Out from which such power proceedeth! —
Fierce it falls on winter's workings,
And undoes its frost formations:
First it bids the cold snow vanish,
Then unchains the flowing river;
Next the singing streams and brooklets;

Then the long-imprisoned waters
Of the lake beside the mountain.
Soon all things of growing nature,
Too, shall feel these potent forces ;
And the sleeping powers of nature
Clothe the earth with growing beauty.
And all living moving creatures,
Too, shall feel his mystic presence,
While they joy in life and vigor.
    Whence, O Sun ! hast thou thy power ?—
Whence the beauty of this morning ? —
None'but God could e'er have given
Us this morning's beauteous vision,
Or these rapturous thoughts of ours,
With the feelings which they gave us.
O my God ! I thank thee for it, —
For this vision of the morning,
On my soul it is engraven ;
It is *mine*, — 'tis mine forever !

THE BAPTISM OF BLOOD.

It was poured upon Antietam
  Until nature gave a blush,
Where her features, bathed in battle's tide,
  Reposed in evening's hush.

It was poured on red Shiloh,
  In terror's crimson flow,
As if nature caught the parting ray
  Of sunset's crimson glow ;

By the Rappahannock's winding shore,
  Where the burning city's smoke

Hung o'er the field, as if to shield
   With battle's cloudy cloak ;

Till darkness came with tempest clouds,
   As a pall for thousands dead ;
As if the skies with tears would fain
   Wash out the battle's red.

And its rill adown the ramparts ran,
   On Vicksburg's blood-bought forts ;
And still the tide of horror pours
   From James' open courts.

For lo ! again, on Northern soil,
   The purple tide hath ran ;
A *graveyard* fitting altar was
   For the sacrifice of man.

Even pallid demons pause for joy,
   In their imprisoned realms,
To see the tide of wrath disgorged,
   Of mortals whom it whelms.

O God ! how long must this carnage come ?
   How long this crimson flood ?
How long must the noblest dare and die ? —
   Let tears do the work of blood !

Look on the thousand bleeding hearts,
   Which in sorrow now are calmed.
That wait unmurmuring at thy throne,
   With faith in tears embalmed !

Look on the widow left to weep,
   And on the sireless child,
Remembering promises to such,
   Which in thy word have smiled !

Look on thy Church which drifteth
　　To a sin-cursed, ruined home !
Look, and for thine own name's sake
　　Avert this awful doom !

Lord, suffer us to plead with thee ;
　　We will bow before thy throne ;
And while we pray, and plead, we say, --
　　O God, thy will be done !

———•◦∘❋∘◦•———

OUR COUNTRY'S CALL.

Our nation had slumbered, forgetful of fears,
As she felt the strong pulsing of peace-prospered years ;
But warmed in our bosom, and grown by our side,
A foe has been nourished with brotherly pride.

But the mask is now dropped — his visage is bare,
And phœnix-like Tyranny faces us there ;
The blow he has struck, — first, cold-blooded blow,
And Freedom confronteth her eternal foe.

The message : " To Arms ! " by heroes is heard ;
The patriot blood of the country is stirred —
Then rise, sons of freemen, and grapple your cause,
Show tyrants the vigor of Liberty's laws !

Bring forth to the light our forefathers' arms,
Bring, bring to the fight, brothers, but bring them as
　　charms !
The hands that have used them in death are laid low,
But the blood that inspired them continues to flow.

'Tis the life of our kindred; it flushes our homes;
Against *this* the dark current of Tyranny comes!
On their own brave defenders their swords have been
    turned,
And our peace-proffered prayers they have scornfully
    spurned.

Then, forth, brothers, forth! Speed swift to the fray!
Think not they are brothers when freemen they slay!
Can Freedom and Tyranny side by side stand?
Can darkness and light dwell at once in one land?

The truth flashes o'er us, our hearts ache with pain,
As we read, upon facing facts, "Slay or be slain!"
God pity our foes, they have wrought to their harm,
The tempest is swinging "the pine against the palm!"

CARRY CHRIST TO THE HOME BY THE SEA.

The year had waned, and autumn come,
The strife of the season had ceased to hum;
The pomp of summer had passed from view,
And earth was adorned by a mellower hue;
The grand old aisles of the wood by the sea
Taught daily their lessons of earth to me;
The sea, with its ever restless tide,
Ebbed and flowed in solemn pride;
And, as on through watery ways it trod,
Spake of the unseen hand of God.

And the sigh of the sad waves' ceaseless roll
Found answering echo in my soul;
The sigh of the sea in my soul was a sob,
A heavenward yearning tidal throb;

It felt the attracting power of Heaven,
And glad the unseen chain would have riven;
Would have risen above the binding bar,
The fiat found in the words " Thus far ! "
Ah ! why did that soul wave sobbing arise?
Why sad was the sea?   Why sad were the skies?
And what was the burden borne up by that prayer?
What spake that sigh on the autumn air?
I felt, like a fetter, the silken chain,
Bind into my heart that old, old pain !
A soul as pure as nature's may be,
Waited and loved in a home by the sea;
Christ was a stranger, a dear friend, I,
So my soul sobbed responsive to ocean's sigh.

Thus sad was the sea and sad were the skies,
Thus did the tidal prayer arise,
How my soul would have seized, were proffered the power
To bring waters of life to that sea-side flower !
How it chafed like the restless sea on the shore,
It struggled and leapt, to fall back as before ;
To feel and know that God alone,
Through Christ, for our sins, though the least can atone ;
But like as the sea when the storm has ceased,
My soul from surging was soon released ;
A calm came, reflecting a light from above,

That whispered, consolingly, " God is Love."
Though the tumult were stayed, the tide throbbed there,
Reflectingly rising in silent prayer,
An answer came : " A message to *thee*,
Carry Christ to thy friend in the home by the sea."
I gladly read this message of love,
And mingled my mandate with that from above.
There was red on her lip, " love-light in her eye ; "
Her heart unstirred by the seeker's sigh,
As pure as any unsaved can be,
Made laugh and step ever joyous and free ;

But that red lip trembled, a swift swelling tear
Spake the indwelling presence of penitent fear.

*　　*　　*　　*　　*　　*　　*　　*

The charms of salvation were coming to be
'Twined 'round that heart in the home by the sea;
And to nature's abundance there then was given
The charm that fitteth the soul for heaven.
I stand on the shore, she stands by my side,
On the shore that is washed by Eternity's tide;
List! there's the low roar of Eternity's wave,
Let us go forth together the sinner to save;
What nobler or holier aim could there be
Than carrying Christ to all homes by the sea?

CHANGE THE FIGURES.

Again we are through another decade,
　　Which is gone, yet we scarcely know how;
The figures in 'fifty all are made,
Printed and folded, away they are laid,
　　And we must mark 'sixty now;
　　　　Time says, " Change the figures."

What have the figures in 'fifty seen?
　　What the tales they have heard?
Pausing not once to notice the din
　　Lachesis and Clotho have stirred —
　　　　Atropos claims the figures.

Records impartial these figures have kept,
　　And he who wishes may read them; ·
Many, in passing through 'fifty, have slept,
Dreamed they were creeping as on they swept;

Let us bid them awake and heed them,
  The ever-changing figures.

Awakening they'll doubtingly rub their eyes,
  And ask where the records are placed?
Forgetting that ere in the visible skies
The first coming rays of light can arise,
  The invisible arc must be traced,
    Forgetting the arc of figures.

When the light of the Northern aurora they view,
  They think it Aurora the morn;
But flickering auroras grow faint and few,
Then knowing not whence cometh light that's true,
  They even look South for the morn, —
    'Tis wisdom to watch the figures.

The records of 'sixty are just begun,
  But the world is forgetting it fast;
A moment they gaze where Clotho has spun,
Then turn away as though it were done,
  And mingle it with the Past,
    Leaving Wisdom to watch the figures.

It is well for us these figures in life,
  That these same figures must change;
For were it not thus, mid the flurry and strife
With which our living ever is rife,
  To forget of advancing weren't strange.
    'Tis well there's change of "figures."

TO THE AUTHOR OF "JIM BLUDSOE."

BY PLAIN PILGRIM.

I've jist read your story of " Banty Tim ; "
I'm a plain, rough man, but my eyes got dim,
And I never can thank you half-hearty enough,
Though Tilmon's words was a leetle too rough.
But you writ another Bludsoe Jim,
I want more special to speak of him,
In praisin' a life so remarkable loose,
Aint you a-givin' the devil a truce?

I reckon ther' want no such feller ez Jim
That you was paintin', an' made up him,
And to my way of seein', the picter aint true ;
But mebby I take a one-sided view.
Couldn't yer said yer say, an' jest as well,
Without winkin' at things not fit ter tell?
Won't cheap, dirty fellers consider it nice,
An' conclude ther' aint enny such thing ez vice?

Banty Tim won me, and so I write,
Admiration and praise are yours by right ;
But in me they're mixt with suthen of pain,
The reason hereby I hope to explain.
Here's why I shudder at Bludsoe Jim ;
My little boy sees a hero in him,
And I *fear* the model you held in view,
And some way, Dear Col., you *brag on him*, too.

In all your fancies couldn't ye foun'
Some lone Doc Simmons, goin' down
With his train, peering into the darkness grim,
Where death sat motionless watchin' for him?
There's one to sing of, no shadder behind,
And only one wife for directors to find.

Your myth has a meaning that facts won't uphold,
When the real Doc goes down 'tis more truthfully told.

I can't say fluent jest all that I mean,
But *do* make your hero jest decently clean,
Don't drag dirt from the slums into sight,
To give it the halo and mantle of right.
You've a right to some license in making a song,
But he swindles his genius who licenses wrong;
Don't lift up the evil, to cry it to fame,
For the sake of our children, don't glorify shame.

THE SOLDIER'S FAREWELL.

[This poem was the last ever written by Mr. Coan. It was finished and sent to the "Independent Statesman," Concord, N.H., about a week before his death, and was published just as his spirit bade farewell to earth, and went to join the Grand Army in heaven.]   E. J. C.

Once more in my arms would I hold you;
    Once more feel the thrill of your breath;
Once more moved to love would behold you,
    Though I knew the next moment were death.
Come! welcome with red lips inviting,
    Welcome with twining arms;
Hold close, that your dear touch inciting
    May deepen the power of your charms.

Let fear move you not to hinder
    The close touch of clinging kiss;
Let each spark of fire touch tinder
    When we kindle a flame such as this.
All fear and foreboding banish
    With abandon well worthy of bliss,
Pause not to sigh "It will vanish,"
    But deepen with smothering kiss.

Aye, thus, and thus, will I love thee!
　Drive not the delight from your eyes!
Look up thou, for bending above thee,
　My own to your yearning replies.
Our tempest was slow in its coming,
　Swiftly sweet is its rainbow close;
The thrill of its joys benumbing,
　Sits the grief which our parting knows.

Let us float to the drifting of dreams,
　While the rainbow of love bends o'er us
As the calm light royally gleams
　On the glory retreating before us.
How sweet to dream after tasting
　The touch of loves moistening dew,
While the bright glow of love's implanting
　On bosom and face burns through!

Let us turn for a moment,— forgetful
　Of all but joy's tropical skies,
With no thought of clouds, gray and fretful,
　To scorn the bright dreams that arise.
Under arches of forests olden,
　Soothed ever by tropical balms,
When day has sunset golden
　Unstirred by war's alarms.

And the low lisping murmur of waters
　Kissing ever the silvery sand,
While naiads, the fay's sea-daughters,
　Disport in our dream on the strand.
But 'waken! once more behold me!
　Your eyes are in dreamy eclipse;
See, close in my arms I hold thee,
　And plead the reply of your lips!

Once more prove thy title well given,
　" Queen Lover," and ever to thee,

When the bolt of battle hath riven
　　Our lives, my thoughts shall flee.
Entwine with arms that cling ever;
　　Let thy red lips part for my kiss;
Thou hast thrilled me before, but never
　　As this agony tinging our bliss.

But the summons " To arms ! " is sounding,
　　From love, perchance life, I must part;
Soon again will my pulse be bounding,
　　Not as now from the warmth of my heart;
But clear through the danger of battle
　　Shall come the sweet sound of your sigh;
Through the sound of the musketry's rattle
　　I'll hear it if fate bids me die.

From life and the joy of loving,
　　From all that men hold dear,
They went out their loyalty proving,
　　Unhindered by joy or fear.
They sleep well, who went to return not;
　　And those who in peace returned,
Met the welcome that waited, to turn not
　　From the brave who that welcome had earned.

PART III.

PART III

AHMAIDEE,

A LYRIC ROMANCE,

BY

REV. LEANDER S. COAN.

Author of "Better in the Mornin'," "England in the Orient,"
"Old Corporal Ballads," etc.

PREFACE.

The effort of American women to provide the privileges of higher education to the women of ancient Haiasdani,[1] known as Armenia to us, has in it the elements of Romance that find fitting field for development in that region of the origin of the human race, and of its most tragical and touching histories. I have striven to weave legend and history largely into my story of that ancient, once martial, always beautiful race, whence the European families of nations had their origin. The scene of the poem proper is laid in Haiasdani in the year 1604. The legend is supposed to be related by a Caucasian girl in the College for Women at Harpoot, to a young lady companion, a daughter of her instructress. She is called Ahmaidee, for the heroine of the legend, from whom she is descended. I have not the hardihood to suppose I have written a great lyric. But if the blending of the sober and tragical elements of history and tradition with this light fancy I have woven shall tend to awaken an interest in Ahmaidee's race, and in the endeavor to provide them with the privileges of a higher education, some good may be accomplished.

> Go forth, fond dream of that people
>   Whence our own life-blood flows;
> Go, sing to the thoughtful and waken
>   To thoughts of these lyric dreams;
> Go forth with purpose as pure
>   As the air o'er Caucasus snows, —
> Singing to those o'er whom once more
>   The Star of the Morning gleams.

L. S. C.

AHMAIDEE.

Ahmaidee, a maid of Caucasus,
   Sits, at the twilight hour,
By the side of a child of the missions,
   In Haiasdanian bower.
The toils of the day are over;
   In an Eden evening sun
They dream their dreams together,
   When the day's toils all are done.
Ahmaidee, a maid of the mountains,
   Bearing in form and face
Those lines of matchless beauty
   Which still adorn her race, —
A race whose dim traditions
   Trace through chaotic years
To Patriarch Togarmah,[2] —
   As the child at knee still hears, —
Whose honored grandsire, Japhet,
   On a mount in Haiasdani stood
When he, with his father's household,
   Alone escaped from the flood.

And there in the land of Eden,
   In Harpoot's[3] college walks,
The maid of Caucasus muses,
   And with sweet simplicity talks
Of the legends and loves of her people,
   In return for the classic lore
Which devout and earnest woman
   Has brought to Armenia's shore.

In that land, the dream of the poet,
    Haiasdani, Eden clime,
To a people crushed, submissive,
    The truth returns at last;
And they sit, in reverent wonder
    That the refluent wave sublime
Returns where its living waters
    First laved the storied past.

And I will tell you the legend
    That our modern Ahmaidee told,
Her eyes, so wistful, pleading,
    With the look of a startled fawn;
And her wealth of woman's glory,
    Just touched with a tinge of gold,
Which the rays of an amber sunset
    Changed not, though they fell upon.

Nor wonder that sultan and caliph
    Seraglio and palace adorn
With these blooms of Caucasian beauty;
    Nor that in marts they are sold
By those robber Koords, their captors;
    Nor that they, dejected, forlorn,
Hear the sound of money-changers,
    And look with disgust on the gold.

For to-day the shah and the sultan,
    In lives of most brutal lust,
With the sanction of Islam's prophet,
    And the law of a tyrant's will,
Crush these flowers of the mountains,
    Trample them into the dust;
And woman's holiest mission
    They lose the right to fulfil.

To be lover, wife, and mother,
    These splendid daughters of earth

May not hope for; but lustful caresses;
  The toy of a revelling hour.
They whom this foul fate seizes
  May never know the worth
Of home, the best joy of woman,
  Nor pure love's blessed dower.

To our Ahmaidee is dawning
  The light of a better day
Than ever arose to her vision
  In the brightest of her dreams
By the side of the river Kura,
  Of Stamboul or Cathay, —
The light of homes which the gospel
  Gilds with its blessed beams.

"Whence was her name, Ahmaidee?"
  The maiden from over the seas
Had asked, and waited the answer.
  The toils of the day were done,
And they strolled in the early evening,
  Fanned by sweet-scented breeze,
For a rest from the Sage of Korene,[4]
  In the rays of the setting sun.

And there, in an arbor resting,
  O'erlooking the nestled town,
By the side of that ancient river
  Which has its source and flows
On through the region of Eden,
  From a mount of a world's renown,
There, as limpid and crystal,
  From Ararat's melting snows,

Not in her broken English,
  Touched by Arminian tongue,
As its musical flow and accent
  In its cadence rose and fell,

Which Haiasdinian poets
Of old so sweetly sung;
I catch but occasional cadence,
When it suiteth my ballad well.

I.

" When the first Grand Caliph Ahmed,[5]
And the great Shah Abbus[6] fought,
To the proud old chief Togarmah,[7]
Of Haiasdinian clan,
The great shah's signal triumph
The fate of a captive brought;
And he with forty thousand
Was carried to Ispahan.

" His only child, Ahmaidee,
The joy of his life and pride,
Was also torn from his castle
With maid and serving-man,
From vineyards and flocks encircling
The grand old mountain side,
Toward Indus, past Kura and Arras,[8]
And the domes of Leukoran.[9]

" Leontius,[10] bard and lover,
With the captives proudly trod,
With look of scornful sadness
On his noble yet youthful face,
And a lingering glance at the mountains,
A reverent step on the sod;
With composure and grace befitting
A noble though conquered race.

" Sadly the caravan journeyed
Many and weary days,

Despoiled their homes and humbled
　Their nation's name and pride.
Persia's luxurious gardens
　Tempt in vain their gaze,
And they wept at sight of the vineyards
　On Elburz's[11] sunward side.

" Southward, past Koom and Teheran,[12]
　Where the victor his pageant displays
To loyal lords and ladies
　And princes of royal line ;
And then the tumult and insult
　Of the rabble's vulgar gaze,
Made wild by the great shah's triumph,
　Inflamed by lust and wine.

" Togarmah, with jewels secreted
　In a hollow sandal string,
Gems whose lustre had glistened
　And gleamed for centuries past ;
From the hands of his fathers descended,
　A ransom fit for a king !
Of that line of mountain princes,
　Alas ! he was the last.[13]

" And during the revel attending
　The great Shah's proud return,
The soul of the old Caucasian,
　Too proud to bear his fate,
Yielded its earthly dwelling,
　And went to his rest to learn
What was a patriot's welcome
　At Paradise's golden gate.

" His blessing to Ahmaidee
　And lover he gravely gave ;
And giving the precious sandals
　Bade them be brave and strong ;

Bade them give him Haikan burial
    In a hidden mountain grave,
And bade them escape with their jewels
    Ere they had journeyed long.

" As they journeyed from Teheran
    On toward Ispahan,
The scattered guarding columns
    Grew riotous in the rear,
Relaxing their martial rigor ; —
    A trader from Seïstan,[14]
For barter with the captives,
    With two fine steeds drew near.

" Their necks like softest satin,
    Their nostrils like pearly shells,
Limbs so slender, and rounding
    Gracefully, strong, and full,
Where the tremulous muscle fibre
    Into haunch and shoulder swells,
And eyes full of fire, yet tender ;
    With a rein you need not pull.

" Those noble steeds the Afghan
    Trader cautiously brought
To the columns of the captives,
    With seeming only to gaze
With an eye of curious wonder ;
    With craft a purchaser sought.
While he left the docile creatures
    To quietly quaff and graze.

" Two suits of Persian texture,
    Such as worn by noble youth,
Leontius had secreted,
    Waiting such time and chance
As fate might bring the watchful ;
    Believing the sacred truth

That ever on those that trust him
   Rests Allah's protecting glance.

" For Islam's faith had invaded
   From the east, the south, and west,
Displacing Nazareth's prophet.
   Though our people still worshipped him,
On the Koran's crude traditions
   Unconscious his thoughts would rest.
Allah was God ; but his knowledge
   And worship were ever sadly dim.

" Bela and Dasti, the Afghan
   Named two of his fairest steeds,
Imported from Djebel Akhdar,[15]
   By ship over Oman sea ;
They are all that brave Leontius,
   Chafing with waiting, needs,
With lover and two attendants,
   To the west by night to flee.

" With cunning craft and foresight
   The Afghan thought in that throng
Might chafe some haughty captive,
   Restive, and rich, and bold,
Who would gladly give price of ransom,
   Nor stand to parley long
Before he would gladly, in silence.
   For the steeds give jewels or gold.

" And he had reckoned wisely ;
   And he clutched with eager hand
The jewel they gave in purchase ;
   Nor more eagerly took than they
The reins on their loving treasures ;
   Nor valued the crystal sand
A moment beside the faithful
   Creatures that sped them away.

THE FLIGHT.

" Away, away, from Ispahan,
  Leaving the range of Astrabad ; ·
Past the vales of Teheran,
  Under the towering Demevad ;
Sighting receding Farsistan ;[16]
  Sighting the hills towards Bagdad,
And the gleam of the sentinel of the Van,
  Away, away, the captives fled,
Petting their panting and foaming steeds
  With as fond caresses
As ever lover with gentle deeds
  The hand of a lover presses,
Wooing and urging the brave and fair,
  The brave, proud steeds who bore them,
Breathing to Allah and God a prayer
  Into the heavens o'er them.
From the life of a slave
  The brave flees ;
From worse than a grave
  The maid who sees
The caliph's grand seraglio,
  With its eunuch grim
Waiting to groom for his master,
  As the groom of his patient steeds,
With caparisons and odors
  And housings for neck and limb,
And then the brute, to his service,
  Dumb and unmurmuring leads.

" And just this fate to thousands
  Of Ahmaidee's race had come ;
And just this fate with horror
  Her whole soul loathed upon ;
While of its fearful terror
  Her maiden lips were dumb,

As she with her valiant lover
To the west was speeding on.

"On the Eastern slope of mountains
.O'erlooking Persia's vales,
They rest them on their journey
Under the mellow stars ;
Rehearsing martial legends,
Romance of olden tales,
Like a true troubadour, Leontius
Sang to unwritten bars,

"And there in the gathering shadows
Unfolded the classic lore
Of Haiasdanian sages,
Poets and holy men,
To wondering Ahmaidee,
Who listened enthralled to his store
Of history and legend,
On the slope of Suliman.[17]

"And one of the tales he told her,
More thrilling than all the rest,
Was the fate of Artavasdes[18]
Sixteen centuries gone ;
That he was conquered and captive
Gave the tale peculiar zest,
And pity for valiant hero
Dying in Egypt alone.

"While love speeds the hour with swifter wings,
Ahmaidee listens while her lover sings.

ARTAVASDES.

"'When the eagles of Rome to Syria came
With Antony, warrior of glorious fame,

Artavasdes, then Haiasdani's lord,
Disputed his progress with banner and sword.

"'He was Syria's master, and fought to retain
The land the Seleucids had fought for in vain, —
This gem in Tigranis's royal crown!
He fought for his kingdom, and not for renown.

"'But the eagles of Rome had iron beaks.
The Haikan tiger vainly seeks
To stay their banners and engines of war,
And Antony's eagles hold Syria.

"'It was thus the last prince of Arsàbid's line
Aided a Syrian laurel to twine
For that Roman's brow, who at Egypt's feet
Lay laurel and sword and armor complete.

"'The king, now a captive, with the captor's proud train,
Through Damascus, along the Dead Sea plain,
Haughtily, sadly, unmurmuring moves
To the scenes of Mark Antony's revels and loves.

"'Alexandria yet was the queen of the sea,
Though broken the Ptolemic dynasty;
For the conquered queen had conquered her lord.
By lances more potent than Roman sword.

"'Her kingdom was man; her love a Nile
Overflowing its banks with passionate wile;
Calling for love's most voluptuous fruit,
Panting, she paused for censure's cold bruit.

"'Then Rome laid his eagles and heart at her feet,
And though she surrenders is victor complete;
And now of his loyalty well to convince
He leads to her throne Haiasdani's prince.

" ' Proud Egypt ne'er brooks an unmelting glance ;
Grand creature of impulse, caprice, and of chance ;
As the haughty prince pleased not that moment's caprice,
All useless are ransom or hope of release.

" ' Into pyramid dungeon, the Haikan lord,
With no need of slave to keep watch and ward ; —
He will furnish no legions, no alliance form,
Though Antony rage, and his queen lover storm.

" ' The axe in the hand of a Nubian slave
Is poised, suspended ; to yield now will save
His life, his throne, and the semblance of power,
And proud Egypt pleads with the prince for an hour.

" ' He yields not nor wavers, though melting her glance ;
Her spell has no power his heart to entrance ;
Aloud then to the slave she angrily calls,
And the axe in his hands unerringly falls.

" ' Back to the revelling, back to the dance,
To billiards 'mid flourish of trumpet and lance ;
And a headless body is floating the while,
Resigned to that monster, the god [19] of the Nile.

" ' And now in her royal and gold-gilded barge,
Canopied, panoplied, floats down the marge
Of the Nile ; and Rome, with fond dalliance led,
Gives never a thought to his captive, dead.

" ' A captive himself, to love and her queen,
He prizes no longer his banner's fair sheen ;
And the queen scorns all conquest, solace, or home,
But the arms and the heart of her lover from Rome.'

" Ahmaidee, the while these numbers
The young bard dreamily sings,

Clasps the hand of the maiden
Who served and with them fled.

"Back over sixteen centuries   .
Her native devotion clings
With pride to the patriot hero,
Haiasdani's royally loyal dead."

———

INTERLUDE.

Lift thy fair face, Caucasus,
    The sun shall follow the star, —
The star of the morning which shineth
    With healing in his beams;
The might of His will is stronger
    Than chains of Sultan or Czar;
And over the heights of thy mountains
    The light of His coming gleams.

II.

"Through the pass in the Caspian mountains
    The captives dare not flee,
But laid their brave course southward,
    Through the vales of the silvery Van;
Braving rather the wilder journey
    South from the central sea,
Though it led along the border
    Of the Koords of Koordistan;

"The wolves in their native mountain
    More fierce than savage beasts,
Who had ravaged the vales of Caucasus,
    Taking captive the tender maid;

As the wolf, their savage namesake,
  On the sheepfold greedily feasts,
Driving with Sultan's seraglio
  A thriving and barbarous trade.

" To Stamboul's tyrant master
    For centuries have been sold
Those suiting his lustful fancy,
    Either bought or captives in war ;
And the captives' grace and beauty
    Measure their price in gold,
And the wish of the helpless victim
    Cares he, nor questions for.

" For days while they had journeyed
    The mounted scouts of the Koord, —
While they by wondrous beauty
    Of valley and mountain glen,
Enthralled by the spell, had loitered,
    By these and love allured —
Were followed, watched in their progress,
    By those wolves in the form of men.

" And just as they sighted the valley
    Of the lovely lakelet Van ;
Just as their hearts were beating
    For what the day would bring,
They hear fierce cry, — a rushing
    From a gorge in the Koordistan ;
Startled from blissful reverie
    As the cries of the robbers ring.

" The jewel they sought was beauty,
    Knowing not the precious store
Of wealth in sandal secreted ;
    They seize, and quickly bind
The maidens, nor pause to capture,
    Nor slay, nor conquer more ;

Then sped through mountain passes
  They knew so well to find.

" But Bela and Dasti, the faithful,
  To Leontius yet remain ;
Through the gorge where Tigres' waters
  Pass through that mountain range,
The captors, flushed and exulting,
  Seek the way of southern plain,
To the sea by Alexandretta,
  Whence they to ship will change.

" Knowing this the bold Leontius
  Speeds swift to a higher pass
Where the waters of Euphrates
  With dalliance seaward flow,
Which through the same range, higher,
  To southward likewise pass,
Enriching the vales of Bagdad ;
  E'en when swollen, sluggish and slow.

" For he trusts by swifter riding
  To be first on Aleppo's plain,
Believing that love and daring,
  With the aid he will secure,
Will wrest the captured princess
  From the agony of the pain,
The bitter, terrible anguish,
  Her pure heart must endure.

" And as he, speeding, rises and falls,
  The heart of the rider lover calls : —
·' On, brave Bela and Dasti !
  On, at your master's will ;
On, for your fair young mistress
  A captive languishes ;
On, with your swiftest paces,
  Steady and strong, until

The fear from her heart and terror
With deliverance vanishes.

"' On, through the vanishing valley,
    Past the receding Van,
To Karput where Euphrates
    Southward quietly flows,
On, down that gorge the river
    Cuts through the Koordistan,
Where Arabia's sun first kisses
    The chill from Ararat's snows.

"' On, brave steeds, bring your master,
    Though foam fleck steaming flanks;
On, though nostrils distended
    Tell of the fearful strain;
On, till your rescued mistress
    Shall kiss and caress her thanks
For bringing her faithful lover
    To stand by her side again.

"' On, and shoes of silver
    Shall grace your feet before;
And gold on those which follow,
    Shall gleam as you spurn the soil;
On, and bring me safely
    To Ahmaidee's side once more,
And I will bless and caress you
    For faithful and splendid toil.'

"Thus, as he sped, Leontius
    His unspoken fancy sang;
And now down the bank of Euphrates
    They turn their panting steeds,
While the feet of their flying coursers
    Out on the night air rang,
Though no lash touch their shoulders,
    Nor flank from sharp spur bleeds.

"And lo! on the plain of Aleppo,
   Reinforced by horse and man,
They wait the slower movement,
   By which they surely know
Would soon come moving westward
   The robbers' caravan,
With never a thought of rescue,
   Moving unguarded and slow.

"Nor wait they in vain their coming,
   Though the lagging hours seem days;
Our bard, in the guise of a merchant,
   The heart of hempen weed,
Nargileh, and scented spices,
   Temptingly there displays;
Nor passes a single horseman
   Without his closest heed.

"At length his search is rewarded:
   The captive with surprise
Beholds her faithful Dasti,
   And knows her deliverer near;
She waves white hand as he passes,
   And he to the sign replies,
Though the only speech they utter
   Is that which the heart may hear.

"One drug the merchant carries
   More potent than iron chains,
Than even Arabia's hashish, —
   The demon of Cathay,
Whose curse unrelenting clingeth
   Where the white blood of poppy stains,
And over its slaves holds ever
   Demoniac and deepening sway.

"And stronger than greed or caution
   Their love for the baneful thing,

They welcome without suspicion
Or thought of danger near,
Because to sensual revels
The stores of the trader bring,
Appetite's power disarms them
And lulls all warning fear.

"While the robbers disarmed for revel,
Bound by the magic spell,
Dream their enticing visions
So near the shores of the sea,
Leontius watches their progress,
Marking the sleepers well;
That again with fair Ahmaidee
Bela and Dasti may flee.

"The pale moon crescent lingers
On the eve of Arabian night,
O'er hill and valley shedding
Its mellow, silvery beams;
No living thing is moving
In the watcher's wary sight;
And deeper the breath of the sleepers
And deeper the trance of dreams.

"Saddled the steeds and waiting
For the master's cautious sign;
Ahmaidee, wakeful and watching,
The signal agreed upon;
When over the mosque in Aleppo
The moon's rays fall in line,
And from that place of worship
Straight o'er the sleepers shone,

"With cautious, muffled footsteps,
Past sleepers in the tent,
The captive maidens swiftly
Pass curtain and sleeping guard,

Believing that ere the flying
    Hours of the night are spent,
She will rest again, protected
    By the blade of her lover bard.

"On again, Bela and Dasti,
    On to Euphrates' tide;
On, while master and maiden
    Fleetly in silence speed;
On, for maid and master,
    For life and liberty and ride;
Yea, for a maiden's honor,
    From a grave of the living dead.

"Twelve days had the captives journeyed
    Ere they sighted Aleppo's domes;
In ten the brave Leontius
    In swift impatience and dread;
In ten, for succor and rescue
    From Van by Euphrates comes.
Now the captive rides Dasti northward,
    Alive, from worse than dead.

"Then northward, for freedom flying,
    They pass up Euphrates' vales;
For freedom from Koordish robber,
    For freedom from Sultan's will;
Though their nation's life is broken,
    And fear of the Russ assails,
They will on to Northern Caucasus,
    Where their children pay tribute still.

"Then, from the mouths of the Volga
    To the north of Crimean sea,
Caucasian chiefs and people
    Dwelt on native soil,
Until then, like native mountains
    Lifting head to heaven, free;

But henceforth doomed to oppression,
 To vassalage and toil.

"And there, on the slopes of Caucasus,
 Behind their barrier walls,
As defence from Koordish robber,
 Until seized by the Sclavic race;
Driven from right and title
 To her ancestral halls,
Where she had ruled from childhood,
 With native and royal grace,

"Ahmaidee, whose wondrous beauty
 Legend hath handed down;
Who brought to her lover her jewels,
 Her maiden love, and all
The wealth of regal nature
 Worthy of kingdom and crown, —
Nor once, in coming years,
 Desired her gifts to recall.

"Leontius, crossing the Kura
 At Tiflis, returning sings
The fame of Bela and Dasti,
 And the beauty of his bride;
And time flies swift and blissful,
 On joyous, exulting wings,
As along Caucasus passes
 The bard and the princess ride.

CAUCASIAN MOUNTAIN SONG.

"'Each mountain glen, each towering peak,
 Each lovely lake and quiet glade,
With patriot pride and love I speak, —
 Their fame no tyrant can degrade.

Haiasdani ! Haiasdani !
Thy hills and dales are dear to me.
Though tyrant rule, we will not flee ;
They cannot crush our love for thee.

"'I hie me now to mountain glen,
   Where I will rear my love's abode,
Far from the strifes of warring men,
   Whence we with faithful steeds have rode.
     Haiasdani ! Haiasdani ! ·
     Thy hills and dales are dear to me.
     Though tyrant rule, we will not flee ;
     They cannot crush our love for thee.

"'A home as sweet as poet's dream
   We'll found among Caucasus' hills,
Where heaven's pure air, and sun's clear beam,
   The heart with life's sweet rapture thrills.
     Haiasdani ! Haiasdani !
     Thy hills and vales are dear to me.
     Though tyrant rule, we will not flee ;
     They cannot crush our love for thee.

"'My Arab steeds, my mountain bride,
   The chief Togarmah's choicest gem ;
I wait, whate'er may betide,
   My fate in native hills with them.
     Haiasdani ! Haiasdani !
     Thy hills and vales are dear to me.
     Though tyrant rule, we will not flee ;
     They cannot crush our love for thee.

"'And down through time's swift coming years
   Will teach descendants to recall
Ahmaidee's beauty, peril, fears ;
   And Arab steeds, who saved us all.
     Haiasdani ! Haiasdani !
     Thy hills and vales are dear to me.

Though tyrant rule, we will not flee ;
They cannot crush our love for thee.'

"Then on to old age together,
Founding a home and a name ;
Rearing a noble household
Of pure Caucasian youth,
Well known in the mountain for prowess,
For lives of unsullied fame ;
Known well to mountain peasant
For chivalry and truth.

"Two centuries now are numbered
Since to their final rest
Loyal descendants bore them,
While tears their faces lave,
Obeying with faithful following
Each dying wish or behest ;
Then plant their native acassia
Above their mountain grave.

"Years before, with martial honors,
They had buried their Arab steeds,
With shoes both silvern and golden
From the old chief's precious store ;
Leontius having recounted,
In noble verse, their deeds,
And shod them with gold and silver,
As by the Euphrates he swore.

*　　*　　*　　*　　*　　*　　*　　*

"O lady fair! from western land,
Where never tyrant's will is known,
Where humblest with the proudest stand,
Nor king nor prince imperial won !
When I remember my poor race,
Whence Europe's haughty hosts have come, —

For proudest prince to us must trace,
    Proud Latins, and imperial Rome ! —

"My heart for my people aches and bleeds,
    Their wrongs I burn to redress ;
And pray for valorous days and deeds,
    When czar can no longer oppress,
Nor shah nor sultan with iron heel
    Grind Haiasdani into the dust ;
While our brothers crush the hate they feel
    In silence, because they must."

SURLUDE.

Ahmaidee in silence is weeping
    Both sad and joyful tears,
Her glorious eyes preserving
    The beauty of her race,
Her words revealing a spirit
    Born of heroic years, —
A spirit as purely transparent
    As the light of her luminous face.

NOTES.

NOTES TO AHMAIDEE.

[1] Haiasdani, pronounced Hay-az-da-ni, is the native name of Armenia, and of old it included Caucasus, Armenia in Turkey, and Eastern Armenia, now under the Shah of Persia.

[2] It is an Armenian tradition that they are descended from Haik, a son of Togarmah, who was a grandson of Japhet. The name is thus a national one, and is given in the tale to the father of the heroine of this legend.

[3] *Harpoot*, or *Karput*, a town on the Euphrates, west of Lake Van, the site of a classical college of the American Board for educating natives, having a department for women.

[4] *Moses of Korene*, the best known and most reliable native historian.

[5] *Ahmed*, a foe of Persia in 1604.

[6] *Shah Abbus*. The Shah who conquered Ahmed in 1604, ravaged and laid Armenia waste, carrying 40,000 captives to Ispahan.

[7] *Togarmah*, a character supposed to be among the captives, named for patriarchal ancestor.

[8] *Kura* and *Arras*, two rivers flowing eastward into the Caspian sea, in the valley south of the Caucasus mountains.

[9] *Leukoran*, a city on the western shore of the Caspian sea.

[10] *Leontius*, a national name, and the name of one of their national authors.

[11] *Mt. Elburz*, a lofty peak in the chain south of the Caspian.

[12] *Koom* and *Teheran*, two cities between the Caspian and Ispahan, a city in central Persia.

[13] Haiasdani's political existence ceased with this invasion, in 1604, since which time they have been subject to the Czar, the Sultan, and the Shah. Sèe Dulaurier and Prince Dadian, *Revue des Mondes*, in 1854 and 1867.

[14] A lake and its region between Afghanistan and Persia.

[15] *Djebel Akhdar*, a region in Oman, in Southern Arabia, near the sea of Oman.

[16] *Farsistan*, a mountain range south-west of Ispahan.

[17] *Suliman-yah*, a mountain on the western border of Persia.

[18] *Artavasdes*, King of Haiasdani (who had wrested Syria from the Seleucids), who, in defending Syria in the year 55 B.C., was captured by Mark Antony, and carried to Cleopatra, and was afterward put to death by Egypt's queen. (Armenian History.)

[19] *God of the Nile*. The crocodile, which was sacred to the Egyptians.

NOTE TO SIMON GAREW.

The illustration which accompanies the legend of Simon Garew is from a photograph taken by the author. It is a view in Gulf Glen, Maine, which is situated in Bowdoin College grant, on the Ebemee or Pleasant river. The glen is four miles long, and the river has a fall of eight hundred feet in passing through it. The walls of the glen are from seventy to *three hundred feet* high, and are abrupt on both sides, perpendicular much of the way, and in some cases overhanging. Along the west bank the bluffs are bold and continuous. The best means of approach is through Brownville and Katahdin Iron Works. It is an entirely wild region, and about thirty miles into the veritable Maine woods.

A good road from R.R. station at Milo nearly to the glen.

Haqus. The name the Indians gave the glen.

Gulf. The name the lumbermen gave it. .

This view was published in 1873 in the " New York Graphic," accompanying this legend in prose, by the author of this work. The view is midway of the glen, looking north-west. — L. S. C.

In the autumn of 1876, Mr. Coan, accompanied by his brother, Dr. E. S. Coan, of Garland, Maine, and his only son, Leander K. Coan, again visited the gulf with rifle and fishing-rod, anticipating a pleasant time for recreation and rest from mental labor. It was

> The moon when the leaves were red,

and the view upon the neighboring mountain sides was grandly beautiful, for they are covered nearly to their summit with forest, and the variegated tinges of scarlet, red, yellow, and green painted the scenery as no artist's pen can do.

But, like Garew's last visit,

> That time the face of the full moon
> Shone not on the face in the rock;
> For a storm hung black in the heavens.

*   *   *   *   *   *   *   *   *   *

Singularly enough, Mr. C. and his party had contemplated visiting the spot where Garew made his offering to the Great Spirit, " at the very same hour of the night." This they were unable to accomplish for

> That night the storm was black.   ✺

Mr. C. and his brother made an appointment to visit the place again in three years at

> The moon when the leaves were red;

but at the very time appointed the Great Spirit summoned the author to the happy " hunting grounds in the beautiful beyond." — E. S. C.

.

www.ingramcontent.com/pod-product-compliance
Lightning Source LLC
Chambersburg PA
CBHW020535270326
41927CB00006B/593